Customize
YOUR CROCHET

First published in the United States of America by
Creative Publishing international, a division of
Quarto Publishing Group USA Inc.
400 First Avenue North
Suite 400
Minneapolis, MN 55401
1-800-328-3895
www.creativepub.com
Visit www.Craftside.net for a behind-the-scenes peek at our crafty world!

ISBN: 978-1-58923-885-5

Digital edition published in 2015
eISBN: 978-1-62788-257-6
10 9 8 7 6 5 4 3 2 1

Library of Congress Cataloging-in-Publication Data Available

Technical Editor and Symbol Diagrams: Karen Manthey
Copy Editor: Lori Steinberg
Book Design and Page Layout: Laura McFadden Design, Inc.
Body Type Illustrations: Sharon Hubert Valencia
Photographs: Chris Hubert

Printed in China

INTRODUCTION

Most patterns in books and magazines are designed to fit the Classic Rectangle body shape, because almost half of all women fit this body type. In the first section of this book, Customize the Fit, you will find instructions for four different sweaters. Each sweater uses a different stitch pattern, and each stitch pattern has a different degree of difficulty. The original instructions are written to fit the Classic Rectangle body type, and guidance is given for how to adjust the patterns to fit different body types. Once you learn the concept, you can apply it to most patterns. The examples in this book are cardigans, but the principles work just as well for pullovers. Whatever your size, whatever your body type, the most flattering garments are those that fit you properly.

In the section Finish Like a Pro, you will learn methods for finishing your projects that will give them a neat, flawless look. Aside from the fit, there are often features in patterns that we might like to change or details we might like to add. In Embellish for Personal Flair, you'll find ways to embellish your work, add pockets, or change closures to make your projects truly your own creations.

This book is a guide that will help you crochet garments to fit your measurements and your style, expertly finished so you will be proud to wear them.

Margaret

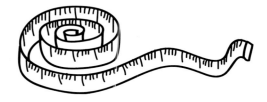

Taking Measurements

Before you begin a project, measure yourself and draw a diagram with your measurements so that you can readily see where the pattern needs to be adjusted. For example, look at the schematics following the sweater patterns on pages 17, 33, 49, and 63. These show the measurements of the final crocheted pieces for each design, assuming one has crocheted in the correct gauge.

HOW TO MEASURE YOUR BODY

Take your measurements over undergarments for accuracy, using a flexible tape measure. Enlist the help of a friend. When measuring the chest, waist, and hips, make sure to keep the tape measure parallel to the floor all around.

1 Chest/Bust. Place the tape measure under the arms, across the widest part of the back and fullest part of the chest/bust line.

2 Waist. Tie a string or piece of narrow elastic around your middle and allow it to roll to your natural waistline. Measure at this exact location. Leave the string in place as a reference for measuring the hips and back waist length.

3 Hips. Measure around the fullest part.

4 Back Waist Length. Measure from the prominent bone at the base of the neck down to the waistline string.

5 Cross Back. Measure from one shoulder crest across the back to the other.

6 Sleeve Length. Take two measurements here: With your arm at your side, measure from the shoulder crest to the wrist bone. Then, with your arm slightly away from your body, measure from the armpit to the wrist.

7 Sleeve Diameter. Measure around the fullest part of your upper arm.

Adjusting Sleeve Measurements

If you have a slightly wider upper arm measurement than the pattern calls for there are a few things that you can do to correct the problem.

First, you must determine how the sleeve pattern increases. Generally the increases are about every two inches (five centimeters), gradually shaping from a cuff to the upper arm. If you need more room in the upper arm area, you can make more increases by placing the increase rows closer together, say about every one and one half inch (four centimeters), until you reach the desired width. You will then have to decrease the added stitches in the cap area. The difficulty of the pattern and the multiple of stitches will determine how to make the increases.

Diagrams are given for how to make increases and decreases for each of the stitch patterns used in the four designs. If you need to make the sleeves longer or shorter than the pattern calls for, this can also be achieved by changing the spacing between increases.

Customize the Fit

My students often tell me that they love to crochet, but they only make things like afghans, baby blankets, scarves, and shawls, because whenever they try to make a garment, it never fits properly.

The first step to making a garment that fits is to understand your body type, and in order to do that you must know how to measure your body correctly.

Included in this section are instructions for four different cardigan sweaters, arranged in order of difficulty based on the stitch pattern. After the basic instructions for each pattern are instructions for how to increase and decrease the stitch pattern, and how to adjust the shape of the sweater to suit different body types. Once you have determined your body type, read through the instructions, choose a project, and pick up your hook. Be patient, check your gauge, and measure often. You can do this!

Understanding Body Types

Most of us fall into one of four main body types:

Classic Rectangle: The hips and chest are balanced and the waist is not deeply defined. This is the most common body type.

TIP *If you are a Rectangle Shape, you may want to give the appearance of a smaller waistline. You can do this by simply decreasing a few stitches at the waist, working for about 2 inches, then increasing back to the original stitch count.*

Triangle (sometimes called Pear Shape): The hips are proportionately larger than the chest and shoulders, and the waist is somewhat defined.

TIP *If you are a Triangle Shape, there are a few things that you can do to balance the hip line and smaller chest. You can add small shoulder pads or add interest, such as a feminine ruffle, to the neckline.*

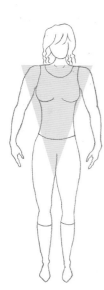

Inverted Triangle: The upper body is proportionately larger with broad shoulders. This body type has an ample chest and wide back, with slim hips.

TIP *If you are an Inverted Triangle, there are a few things that you can do to create balance. You might like to add a V-neck, or add different edges to the bottom of a garment.*

Hourglass: The chest and hips are well balanced and the waist is very defined. The shoulders align with the hips and the upper body is proportionate in length.

TIP *If you are an Hourglass figure, you might want to embrace your curves, and shape the waistline by increasing and decreasing.*

Double Crochet Lace Cardigan

Double crochet lace is one of the easiest stitch patterns to adjust for fit. This lovely open fabric not only turns a classic cardigan shape into something special: it works up quickly, has a soft drape, and lends itself to further embellishment.

SKILL LEVEL
EASY

CLASSIC RECTANGLE

Yarn: Light (3)

Shown: LB Collection Superwash Merino, 100% Superwash Merino Wool, 306 yds/280 m, 3.5 oz/100 g, 6 (6, 7, 8) skeins #139 Peony

Hooks: G/6 (4.25 mm) and H/8 (5 mm) or sizes to obtain gauge

Gauge: With larger hook, 16 sts and 10 rows in patt = 4" (10 cm).

Notions:

Yarn needle

Five ¾" (19 mm) buttons

Sewing needle and matching sewing thread

Sizes: Small (Medium, Large, X large)

Finished Bust: 34 (37, 40, 43)" (86 [94, 102, 109] cm)

Special Stitches

V-stitch (V-st): *(Dc, ch 1, dc) in same st.*

dc2tog: *Yo, insert hook in next designated st, yo, draw yarn through st, yo, draw yarn through 2 loops on hook] twice, yo, draw yarn through 3 loops on hook.*

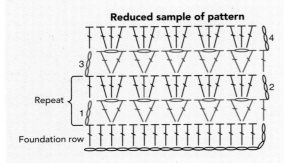

Reduced sample of pattern

Repeat

Foundation row

BACK

With H/8 (5 mm) hook, ch 69 (75, 81, 87).

Foundation Row: Dc in 3rd ch from hook, dc in each ch across, turn. (68 [74, 80, 86] dc).

Row 1: Ch 3 (counts as dc here and throughout), sk first 2 dc, *V-st in next dc, sk next 2 dc, rep from * across to last 2 sts, sk next dc, dc in top of the tch, turn. (22 [24, 26, 28] V-sts; 1 dc on each end).

Row 2: Ch 3, 3 dc in each ch-1 sp across, ending with dc in top of tch, turn.

Rep Rows 1 and 2 until Back measures 12 (12, 12½, 12½)" (30.5 [30.5, 31.5, 31.5] cm) from beg, ending with Row 2 of patt.

Shape Armholes

Row 1: Sl st in each of first 4 dc, ch 3, work Row 1 of patt across to last 5 sts, dc in next dc, turn, leaving rem sts unworked.

Row 2: Ch 3, 2 dc in ch-1 sp of first V-st, 3 dc in each ch-1 sp across row to last ch-1 sp, 2 dc in ch-1 sp of last V-st, dc in top of tch, turn.

Row 3: Ch 3, sk first 2 dc, dc in next dc, work in established patt across to last 4 dc, sk next 2 dc, dc next dc, dc in top of tch, turn.

Row 4: Ch 3, sk first dc, *3 dc in next ch-1 sp, rep from * across to last 2 dc, sk next dc, dc in top of tch, turn.

Row 5: Work in patt Row 1. (18 [20, 22, 24] V-sts)

Work in patt as established until armhole measures 7½ (8, 8½, 9)" (19 [20.5, 21.5, 23] cm) from beg. Fasten off.

LEFT FRONT

With H/8 (5 mm) hook, ch 36 (39, 42, 45).

Foundation Row: Dc in 3rd ch from hook, dc in each ch across, turn. (35 [38, 41, 44] dc)

Work same as Back to Shape Armhole ending with Row 2 of patt.

Shape Armhole

Row 1: Sl st in each of first 4 dc, ch 3, work Row 1 of patt across, turn. (10 [11, 12, 13] V-sts)

Row 2: Work Row 2 of patt across to last ch-1 sp, 2 dc in last ch-1 sp, dc in top of tch, turn. (31 [34, 37, 40] dc)

Row 3: Ch 3, sk first 2 dc, dc in next dc, work in Row 1 patt across, dc in top of tch, turn. (9 [10, 11, 12] V-sts)

Row 4: Ch 3, *3 dc in next V-st, rep from * across to last 2 dc, sk next dc, dc in top of tch, turn.

Row 5: Work in patt Row 1. (9 [10, 11, 12] V-sts)

Work even in patt as established until Armhole measures 6 (6½, 7, 7½)" (15 [16.5, 18, 19] cm) from beg, ending with Row 2 of patt.

Shape Neck

Row 1: Work Row 1 of patt until 5 (5, 6, 6) V-sts are completed, sk next dc, dc in next dc, turn, leaving rem sts unworked.

Work even in patt until armhole measures same as back. Fasten off.

RIGHT FRONT

Work same as Left Front to Shape Armhole, ending with Row 2 of patt.

Shape Armhole

Row 1: Work Row 1 of patt across to last 6 sts, sk next dc, dc in next dc, turn, leaving rem sts unworked.

Row 2: Ch 3, 2 dc in in ch-1 sp of first V-sts, 3 dc in each ch-1 sp across, dc in top of tch, turn.

Row 3: Work in Row 1 of patt across to last 4 dc, sk next 2 dc, dc in next st, 1 dc in top of turning ch, turn. (9 [10, 11, 12] V-sts)

Row 4: Ch 3, sk first dc, 3 dc in each ch-1 sp across row, dc in top of tch, turn. (29 [32, 35, 38] dc)

Work even in patt as established until Armhole measures 6 (6½, 7, 7½)" (15 [16.5, 18, 19] cm) from beg, ending with Row 2 of patt.

Shape Neck

Row 1: Sl st in each of first 12 (15, 15, 18) sts, ch 3, work in Row 1 of patt across, turn. (5 [6, 6, 7] V-sts)

Work even in patt until armhole measures same as back. Fasten off.

Sleeve (make 2)

Note: When measuring the 2½" (6.5 cm) between increase rows, measure after the increase rows are made.

With H/8 hook, ch 39 (39, 42, 42).

Foundation Row: Dc in 3rd ch from hook, dc in each ch across, turn. (38 [38, 41, 41] dc)

Work same as Back until Sleeve measures 3" (7.5 cm) from beg, ending with Row 2 of patt, turn.

First Inc Row: Ch 3, dc in first st, sk next dc, V-st in next dc, *sk next 2 sts, V-st in next st, rep from * across, ending with 2 dc in top of tch, turn. (12 [12, 13, 13] V-sts; 2 dc at each end)

Work even in patt with 2 dc on each end for 5 rows, ending with Row 2 of patt.

Second Inc Row: Ch 3, 2 dc in sp between first 2 sts, *sk next 2 sts, V-st in next st, rep from * across, 2 dc in space between last skipped dc and tch, dc in top of tch, turn. (12 [12, 13, 13] V-sts; 3 dc at each end)

Work even in patt with 2 dc on each end for 5 rows, ending with Row 2 of patt.

Rep First Inc Row. (14 [14, 15, 15] V-sts; 2 dc at each end)

Work even in patt with 2 dc on each end for 5 rows, ending with Row 2 of patt. Rep Second Inc Row. (14 [14, 15, 15] V-sts; 3 dc at each end)

Work even in patt with 2 dc on each end for 5 rows, ending with Row 2 of patt. Rep First Inc Row. (16 [16, 17, 17] V-sts; 2 dc at each end)

Work even in patt with 2 dc on each end until Sleeve measures 16 (16, 16½, 16½)" (40.5 [40.5, 42, 42] cm) from beg, ending with Row 2 of patt.

Shape Cap

Row 1: Sl st in each of first 4 sts, ch 3, work Row 1 of patt across last 5 sts, dc in next dc, turn, leaving rem sts unworked. (14 [14, 15, 15] V-sts)

Row 2 (dec row): Ch 3, 2 dc in first V-sts, 3 dc in each ch-1 sp across row to last ch-1 sp, 2 dc in last ch-1 sp, dc in top of turning ch, turn.

Row 3 (dec row): Ch 3, sk first 2 dc, dc in next dc, work in Row 1 of patt as established across to last 4 dc, sk next 2 dc, dc next dc, dc in top of tch, turn.

Row 4: Ch 3, sk first 3 dc, 3 dc in each ch-1 sp across to last 3 dc, sk next 2 dc, dc in top of tch, turn.

Row 5: Work Row 1 of patt.

Rep Rows 2–5 twice. Fasten off.

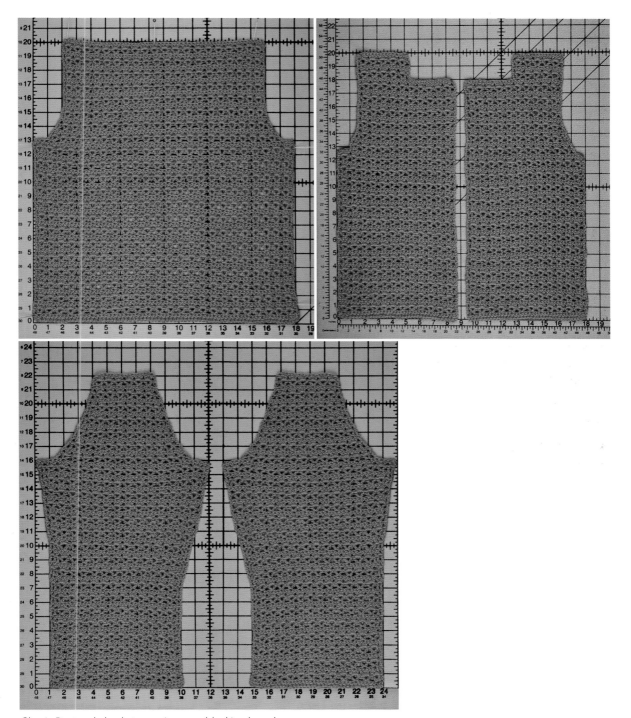

Classic Rectangle body type: pieces on blocking board

ASSEMBLY

Sew shoulder seams. Mark center of Sleeve Cap. Matching center of sleeve cap to shoulder seam and matching bound-off armhole edges, pin in place, easing cap around shoulder. Sew in place. Sew underarm seams.

Neck and Front Border

Note: Before starting border, it is a good idea to mark fronts in 4 equal parts, then work an equal number of sts in each section.

Row 1: With RS facing, join yarn with sl st in bottom Right Front corner, ch 1, work 80 (80, 84, 84) sc evenly spaced across to top corner of Right Front, work 3 sc in corner, working along neck edge, sk next st, work 14 (14, 15, 15) sc across top neck edge, sk next st, work 8 (8, 9, 9) sc evenly spaced across row-end sts to shoulder, sc in each st across back neck edge, work 8 (8, 9, 9) sc evenly spaced across row-end sts to top of neck edge, work 14 (14, 15, 15) sc evenly spaced across to next corner, sk next st, 3 sc in corner, work 80 (80, 84, 84) sc evenly spaced across to bottom Left Front corner, turn.

Row 2: Ch 1, sc in each sc across to next corner, 3 sc in corner st, sk 1 st, sc in each st across to 1 st before next corner st, sk 1 st, 3 sc in corner st, sc in each st across to bottom corner, turn.

Row 3 (buttonhole row): Ch 1, sc in each of next 14 (14, 17, 17) sc, [ch 3, sk 2 sc, sc in each of the next 14 sc] 4 times, ch 3, sk next 2 sc, 3 sc in last sc to turn corner, sk 1 sc, sc in each st across to 1 st before next corner st, sk 1 st, 3 sc in next st, sc in each st across to bottom, turn.

Row 4: Ch 1, sc in each st across to next corner st, 3 sc in corner st, sk 1 st, sc in each st across to 1 st before corner st, sk 1 st, 3 sc in corner, [sc in each st across to next ch-3 sp, 2 sc in next ch-3 space] 3 times, sc in each across to next corner, turn.

Row 5: Rep Row 2, do not turn.

Row 6: Ch 1, working from left to right, reverse sc in each st across. Fasten off.

FINISHING

With sewing needle and thread, sew buttons to Left Front opposite buttonholes.

Blocking: Lay garment on a padded surface and sprinkle with water. Pat into shape. Pin out to measurements using rustproof pins. Allow to dry.

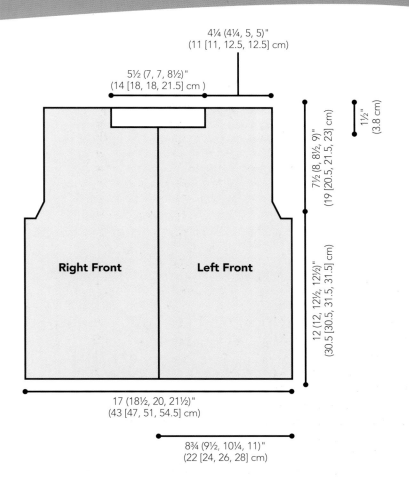

4¼ (4¼, 5, 5)"
(11 [11, 12.5, 12.5] cm)

5½ (7, 7, 8½)"
(14 [18, 18, 21.5] cm)

1½"
(3.8 cm)

7½ (8, 8½, 9)"
(19 [20.5, 21.5, 23] cm)

Right Front

Left Front

12 (12, 12½, 12½)"
(30.5 [30.5, 31.5, 31.5] cm)

17 (18½, 20, 21½)"
(43 [47, 51, 54.5] cm)

8¾ (9½, 10¼, 11)"
(22 [24, 26, 28] cm)

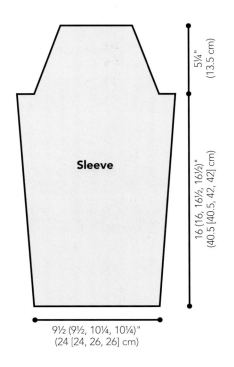

5¼"
(13.5 cm)

Sleeve

16 (16, 16½, 16½)"
(40.5 [40.5, 42, 42] cm)

9½ (9½, 10¼, 10¼)"
(24 [24, 26, 26] cm)

Customizing the Fit

SHAPING DOUBLE CROCHET LACE

V-stitch (V-st): (Dc, ch 1, dc) in same st.

dc2tog: [Yo, insert hook in next designated st, yo, draw yarn through st, yo, draw yarn through 2 loops on hook] twice, yo, draw yarn through 3 loops on hook.

Ch 28.

Foundation Row: Dc in 4th ch from hook (beg ch-3 counts as dc), dc in each ch across, turn. (26 dc)

Row 1: Ch 3 (counts as dc, here and throughout), sk next dc, V-st in next dc *sk next 2 dc, V-st in next dc; rep from * across to last 2 sts, dc in top of tch, turn. (8 V-sts)

Row 2: Ch 3, 3 dc in each ch-1 sp across, dc in top of tch.

Rep Rows 1 and 2 for patt, ending with Row 2 of patt to begin increasing.

Increase and Decrease Pattern

Row 1 (inc row): Ch 3, dc in first st, sk next dc, V-st in next st, *sk next 2 dc, V-st in next dc; rep from * across to last 2 sts, sk next dc, 2 dc in top of tch, turn. (8 V-sts)

Row 2 (inc row): Ch 3, 2 dc in sp between first 2 sts, 3 dc in each ch-1 sp across, sk next 2 dc, 2 dc in sp between last skipped dc and tch, dc in top of tch, turn. (30 dc)

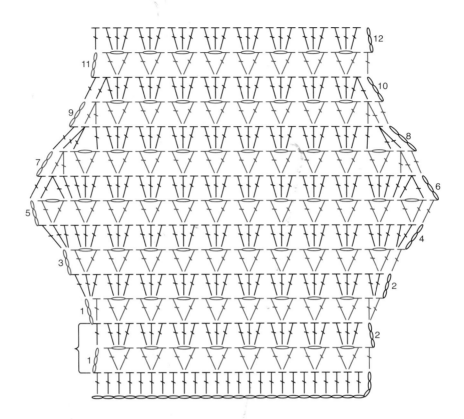

Row 3 (inc row): Ch 3, dc in first st, V-st in next st, *sk next 2 dc, V-st in next dc; rep from * across to last st, 2 dc in top of tch, turn. (10 V-sts)

Row 4 (inc row): Ch 3, 2 dc in sp between first 2 sts, 3 dc in each ch-1 sp across, sk next dc, 2 dc in sp between last skipped dc and tch, dc in top of tch, turn. (36 dc)

Row 5: Ch 3 (counts as dc, here and throughout), V-st in next dc *sk next 2 dc, V-st in next dc; rep from * across to last st, dc in top of tch, turn. (12 V-sts)

Row 6 (dec row): Ch 3, dc2tog over next 2 dc of V-st, dc in next dc, 3 dc in each ch-1 sp across to last 6 sts, dc in next dc, dc2tog over 2 dc of next V-st, dc in in top of tch, turn.

Row 7 (dec row): Ch 3, dc2tog over next 2 sts, sk next st, V-st in next st, *sk next 2 sts, V-st in next st; rep from * across to last 4 sts, sk next st, dc2tog over next 2 sts, dc in top of tch, turn.

Row 8 (dec row): Ch 3, dc2tog over next 2 dc, sk next ch-1 sp, dc in next dc, 3 dc in each ch-1 sp across to last 7 sts, dc in next dc, sk next ch-1 sp, dc2tog over next 2 dc, dc in in top of tch, turn. (30 sts)

Row 9: Rep Row 7. (8 V-sts)

Row 10 (dec row): Ch 3, dc2tog over next 2 dc, 2 dc in next ch-1 sp, 3 dc in each ch-1 sp across to last 6 sts, 2 dc in last ch-1 sp, dc2tog over next 2 dc, dc in in top of tch, turn. (26 sts)

Rows 11 and 12: Work even in patt.

THE TRIANGLE BODY

If your body type is Triangle, begin your garment following a size that fits your hip measurement, then gradually decrease to fit the waist and chest measurements of a smaller size. Once you have reached your chest measurement, finish the garment following the smaller size instructions.

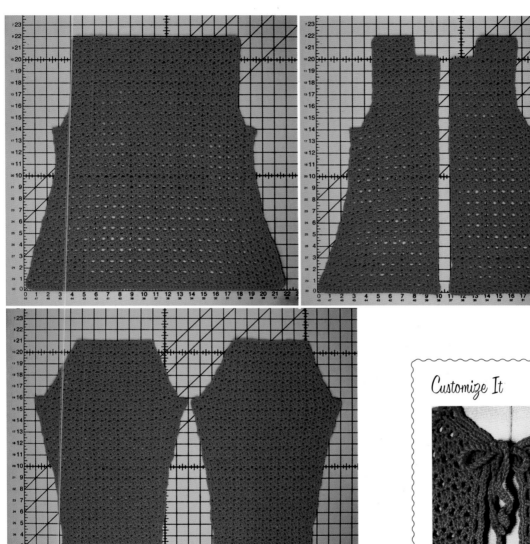

Triangle body type: pieces on blocking board

Customize It

To customize the style of this sweater and add interest at the neckline, a Simple Scallop Edging (page 101) and a chain tie at the neck for fastening are used.

THE INVERTED TRIANGLE

If your body type is Inverted Triangle, begin your garment following a size that fits your hip measurement, then gradually increase to the waist and chest measurement of a larger size. Once you have reached your chest measurement, finish the garment following the larger size instructions.

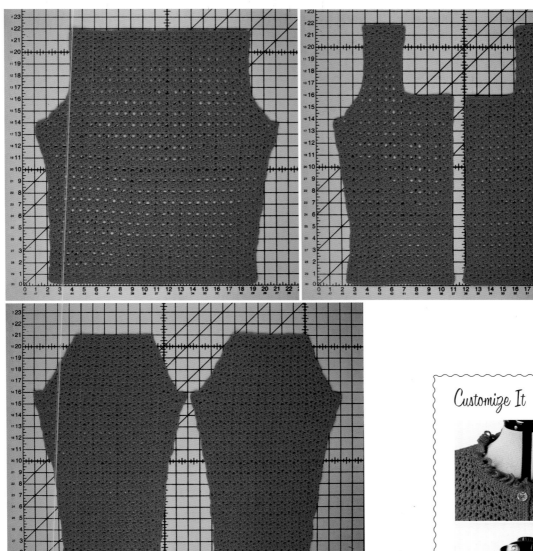

Inverted Triangle body type: pieces on blocking board

Customize It

To customize the style of this sweater, the neckline was lowered and trimmed with the Contessa Ruffle (page 100).

THE HOURGLASS

If your body type is Hourglass, begin your garment following a size that fits your hip measurement, then gradually decrease to your waist measurement; work about 2 inches (5 centimeters) even, then gradually increase to your chest measurement. Once you have reached your chest measurement, finish the garment following the size that fits your chest measurement.

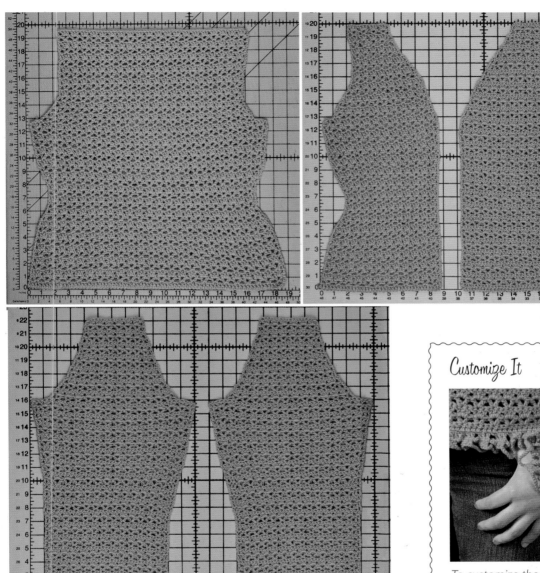

Hourglass body type: pieces on blocking board

To customize the style of this sweater, a V-shape neckline was worked (see shaping DC Lace, page 18), and the Contessa Ruffle (page 100) was added to the bottom and sleeve edges.

Bobbles and Bars Cardigan

Bobbles and Bars is a pattern that will test your crochet skills. While not the easiest of stitch patterns, it does produce a very impressive fabric, and when you finish this cardigan, your friends will be asking "did you really make that?" I have included two different methods for shaping this pattern, and these methods also work for other patterns with similar stitch combinations.

SKILL LEVEL
EXPERIENCED

CLASSIC RECTANGLE

Yarn: Light (3)

Shown: LB Collection Superwash Merino, 100% Superwash Merino Wool, 306 yds/280 m, 3.5 oz/100 g, 6 (6, 7, 8) skeins #174 Spring Leaf

Hooks: F/4 (3.75 mm) and G/6 (4 mm) or sizes to obtain gauge

Gauge: With larger hook, 18 dc and 10 rows in patt = 4" (10 cm).

Notions

Yarn needle

Five ¾" (19 mm) buttons

Sewing needle and matching sewing thread

Sizes: Small (Medium, Large, X large)

Finished Bust: 34 (38, 42, 46)" (86.5 [96.5, 106.5, 117] cm).

Special Stitches

Bobble: *Working over the post of previous dc, [Yo, pick up a loop, yo, draw yarn through 2 lps on hook] 5 times, yo, draw yarn through all 6 loops on hook.* **Note:** *Bobbles must be worked loosely. If worked too tightly they tend to go to the wrong side of work. They can be pushed gently to the right side of work.*

V-stitch (V-st): *(Dc, ch 1, dc) in same st or sp.*

Front Post double crochet (FPdc): *Yo, insert hook from front to back to front again around the post of next st, yo, draw yarn through st, [yo, draw yarn through 2 loops on hook] twice.*

Back Post double crochet (BPdc): *Yo, insert hook from back to front to back again around the post of next st, yo, draw yarn through st, [yo, draw yarn through 2 loops on hook] twice.*

Reduced Sample of Pattern

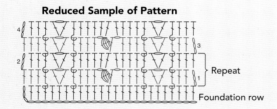

Ch a multiple of 2 plus 1.

Foundation Row: Dc in 4th ch from hook, dc in each ch across, turn.

Row 1: Ch 3 (counts as dc, here and throughout), sk first st, dc in each of the next 2 dc, *FPdc around the post of next st, sk next st, V-st in next st, sk next dc, FPdc around the post of next st**, dc in each of next 3 sts, ch 1, sk next st, dc in next st, bobble around the post of last dc made, ch 1, sk next st, dc in each of next 3 sts, rep from * across, ending last rep at **, dc in each of next 2 sts, dc in top of tch, turn.

Row 2: Ch 3, sk first st, dc in each of next 2 sts, *BPdc around the post of next st, V-st in ch-1 sp of next V-st, BPdc around the post of next st**, dc in each of next 3 sts, dc next ch-1 sp, dc in next bobble, dc in next ch-1 sp, dc in each of next 3 sts, rep from * across, ending last rep at **, dc in each of next 2 sts, dc in top of tch, turn.

Rep Rows 1 and 2 for patt.

BACK

With G/6 (4 mm) hook, ch 83 (91, 99, 107).

Foundation Row: Dc in 4th ch from hook, dc in each ch across, turn. (81 [89, 97, 105] dc)

Row 1 (RS): Ch 3 (counts as dc, here and throughout), sk first st, dc in each of the next 2 (6, 10, 14) dc, *FPdc around the post of next st, sk next st, V-st in next st, sk next dc, FPdc around the post of next st, dc in each of next 3 sts, ch 1, sk next st, dc in next st, bobble around the post of last dc made, ch 1, sk next st, dc in each of next 3 sts, rep from * 4 times, FPdc around the post of next st, sk next st, V-st in next st, sk next st, FPdc around the post of next st, dc in each of next 2 (6, 10, 14) sts, dc in top of tch, turn. (5 bobble sections; 6 FPdc sections, 3 (7, 11, 15) dc on each end.

Row 2: Ch 3, sk first st, dc in each of next 2 (6, 10, 14) sts, *BPdc around the post of next st, V-st in ch-1 sp of next V-st, BPdc around the post of next st, dc in each of next 3 sts, dc next ch-1 sp, dc in next bobble, dc in next ch-1 sp, dc in each of next 3 sts, rep from *

4 times, BPdc around the post of next st, V-st in ch-1 sp of next V-st, BPdc around the post of next st, dc in each of next 2 (6, 10, 14) dc, dc in top of tch, turn.

Rep Rows 1 and 2 until piece measures 12 (12, 12½, 12½)" (30.5 [30.5, 31.5, 31.5] cm) from beg, ending with Row 1 of patt.

Shape Armholes

Row 1: Sl st in each of first 5 (6, 7, 8) sts, ch 3, maintaining patt as established, work in patt Row 2 across to within last 4 (5, 6, 7) sts, working dc sts at beg and end of row when patt is not complete, turn, leaving rem sts unworked. (73 [79, 85, 91] sts)

Maintaining patt as established, dec 1 st at each end of every row (4 [4, 5, 5] times).

Work even in patt until armhole measures 8 (8½, 9, 9½)" (20.5 [21.5, 23, 24] cm) from beg. Fasten off.

RIGHT FRONT

With G/6 (4 mm) hook, ch 41 (45, 49, 53).

Foundation Row: Dc in 4th ch from hook, dc in each ch across, turn. (39 [43, 47, 51] dc)

Row 1 (RS): Ch 3, sk first dc, dc in each of the next 2 sts, *FPdc around the post of next st, sk next st, V-st in ch-1 sp of next V-st, sk next st, FPdc around the post of next st, dc in each of next 3 sts, ch 1, sk next st, dc in next st, bobble around the post of last dc made, ch 1, sk next st, dc in each of next 3 dc, rep from * once, FPdc around the post of next st, sk next st, V-st in next st, sk next st, FPdc around the post of next st, dc in each of next 2 (6, 10, 14) sts, dc in top of tch, turn. (2 bobble sections; 3 FPdc sections; 3 (7, 11, 15) dc on armhole end.

Row 2: Ch 3, sk first st, dc in each of the next 2 (6, 10, 14) sts, *BPdc around the post of next st, V-st in ch-1 sp of next V-st, BPdc around the post of next st, dc in each of next 3 sts, dc in next ch-1 sp, dc in next bobble, dc in next ch-1 sp, dc in each of next 3 dc, rep

from * once, BPdc around the post of next st, V-st in ch-1 sp of next V-st, BPdc around the post of next st, dc in each of next 2 sts, dc in top of tch, turn.

Rep Rows 1 and 2 until piece measures 12 (12, 12½, 12½)" (30.5 [30.5, 31.5, 31.5] cm) from beg, ending with Row 1 of patt.

Shape Armhole

Row 1: Sl st in each of first 5 (6, 7, 8) sts, ch 3, maintaining patt as established, work in patt Row 2 across, turn. (35 [38, 41, 44] sts)

Maintaining patt as established, dec 1 st at armhole end of every row (4 [4, 5, 5] times). (31 [34, 36, 39] sts)

Work even in patt until armhole measures 6 (6½, 7, 7½)" (15 [16.5, 18, 19] cm) from beg. Fasten off.

SHAPE NECK

Next Row: Work in patt as established across first 17 (19, 21, 23) sts, turn, leaving rem stitches unworked. Work even in patt until armhole measures same as Back. Fasten off.

LEFT FRONT

With G/6 (4 mm) hook, ch 41 (45, 49, 53).

Foundation Row: Dc in 4th ch from hook, dc in each ch across, turn. (39 [43, 47, 51] dc)

Row 1: Ch 3, sk first st, dc in each of the next 2 (6, 10, 14) sts, *FPdc around the post of next st, sk next st, V-st in next st, sk next st, FPdc around the post of next dc, dc in each of next 3 sts, ch 1, sk next st, dc in next st, bobble around the post of last dc made, ch 1, sk next st, dc in each of next 3 sts, rep from * once, FPdc around the post of next st, sk next st, V-st in next st, sk next st, FPdc around the post of next dc, dc in each of next 2 sts, dc in top of tch, turn. (2 bobble sections; 3 FPdc sections; 3 [7, 11, 15] dc at armhole side)

Row 2: Ch 3, sk first st, dc in each of the next 2 sts, *BPdc around the post of next st, V-st in ch-1 sp of next V-st, BPdc around the post of next st, dc in each of next 3 sts, dc next ch-1 sp, dc in next bobble, dc in next ch-1 sp, dc in each of next 3 sts, rep from * once, BPdc around the post of next st, V-st in ch-1 sp of next V-st, BPdc around the post of next st, dc in each of the next 2 (6, 10, 14) sts, dc in top of tch, turn.

Rep Rows 1 and 2 until piece measures 12 (12, 12½, 12½)" (30.5 [30.5, 31.5, 31.5] cm) from beg, ending with Row 1 of patt.

Shape Armhole

Row 1: Work in patt as established across to within last 4 (5, 6, 7) sts, turn, leaving rem sts unworked.

Maintaining patt as established, dec 1 st at armhole end of every row (4 [4, 5, 5] times). (31 [34, 36, 39] sts)

Work even in patt until armhole measures 6 (6½, 7, 7½)" (15 [16.5, 18, 19] cm) from beg. Fasten off.

Shape Neck

Sl st in each of first 15 (16, 16, 17) sts, ch 3, work in patt across rem 17 (19, 21, 23) sts, turn. Work even in patt until armhole measures same as Back. Fasten off.

SLEEVE (MAKE 2)

With G/6 (4 mm) hook, ch 41 (45, 49, 53).

Foundation Row: Dc in 4th ch from hook, dc in each ch across, turn. (39 [43, 47, 51] dc)

Work even in patt same as Back for 2" (5 cm).

Maintaining patt as established, forming new patterns as sts are increased, inc 1 st at each end of every row 12 times. Work even until Sleeve measures 15½ (16, 16½, 17)" (39.5 [40.5, 42, 43] cm) from beg, ending with Row 1 of patt. (63 [67, 71, 75] sts)

Shape Cap

Row 1: Sl st in each of first 6 sts, ch 3, work in patt across to last 5 sts, turn, leaving rem sts unworked. (53 [57, 61, 65] sts)

Row 2: Ch 3, sk next st, work in patt across to last 2 sts, sk next st, dc in top of tch, turn. (51 [55, 59, 63] sts)

Row 3: Ch 3, [dc2tog over next 2 sts] twice, work in patt across to within last 5 sts, [dc2tog over next 2 sts] twice, dc in top of tch, turn. (47 [51, 55, 59] sts)

Row 4: Ch 3, dc2tog over next 2 sts, work in patt across to within last 3 sts, dc2tog over next 2 sts, dc in top of tch, turn. (45 [49, 53, 57] sts)

Rows 5–11: Rep Row 4. Fasten off. (31 [35, 39, 43] sts)

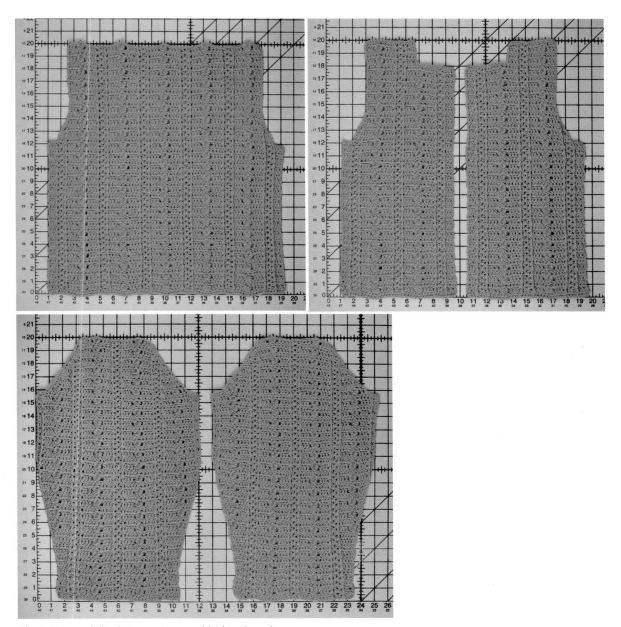

Classic Rectangle body type: pieces on blocking board

ASSEMBLY

Sew shoulder seams. Mark center of Sleeve Cap. Matching center of cap to shoulder seam and matching bound-off armhole edges, pin in place, easing cap around shoulder. Sew in place. Sew underarm seams.

Neck and Front Border

Row 1: With RS facing and F/5 (3.75 mm) hook, join yarn at bottom Right Front corner, ch 1, work 80 (82, 84, 86) sc evenly spaced across to top corner of Right Front, work 3 sc in corner, work 22 (24, 26, 28) sc evenly spaced across to shoulder seam, sc in each st across back neck edge to shoulder seam, work 22 (24, 26, 28) sc evenly spaced across to top of Left Front corner, work 3 sc in corner, work 80 (82, 84, 86) sc evenly spaced across to bottom Left Front corner, turn.

Row 2: Ch 1, sc in each sc across to next corner, 3 sc in corner st, sk 1 st, sc in each st across to 1 st before next corner st, sk 1 st, 3 sc in corner st, sc in each st across to bottom corner, turn.

Row 3 (buttonhole row): Ch 1, sc in each of first 8 (10, 8, 10) sc, [ch 3, sk next 2 sts, sc in each of next 15 (15, 16, 16) sc] 4 times, ch 3, sk next 2 sts, sc in each sc across to next corner st, 3 sc in corner st, sk 1 st, sc in each st across to 1 st before next corner st, sk 1 st, 3 sc in corner st, sc in each st across to bottom corner, turn.

Row 4: Ch 1, sc in each st across to next corner, 3 sc in corner st, sk 1 st, sc in each st across to 1 st before corner st, sk 1 st, 3 sc in corner, [sc in each st across to next ch-3 sp, 2 sc in next ch-3 space] 5 times, sc in each across to next corner, turn.

Row 5: Rep Row 2. Fasten off.

FINISHING

With sewing needle and thread, sew buttons to Left Front opposite buttonholes.

Blocking: Lay garment on a padded surface and sprinkle with water. Pat into shape. Pin out to measurements using rustproof pins. Allow to dry.

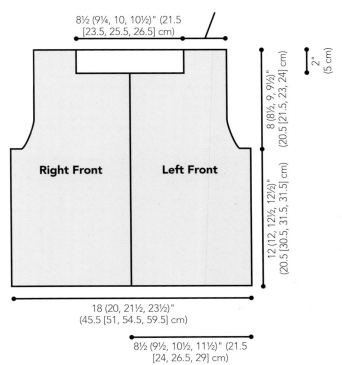

3¾ (4¼, 4½, 5)"
(9.5 [11, 11.5, 12.5] cm)

8½ (9¼, 10, 10½)" (21.5
[23.5, 25.5, 26.5] cm)

2"
(5 cm)

8 (8½, 9, 9½)"
(20.5 [21.5, 23, 24] cm)

Right Front

Left Front

12 (12, 12½, 12½)"
(20.5 [30.5, 31.5, 31.5] cm)

18 (20, 21½, 23½)"
(45.5 [51, 54.5, 59.5] cm)

8½ (9½, 10½, 11½)" (21.5
[24, 26.5, 29] cm)

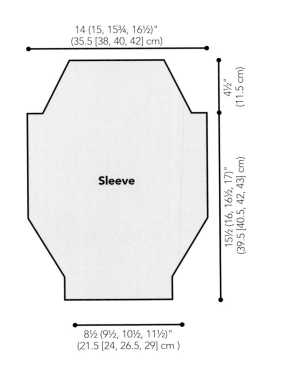

14 (15, 15¾, 16½)"
(35.5 [38, 40, 42] cm)

4½"
(11.5 cm)

Sleeve

15½ (16, 16½, 17)"
(39.5 [40.5, 42, 43] cm)

8½ (9½, 10½, 11½)"
(21.5 [24, 26.5, 29] cm)

Customizing the Fit

SHAPING BOBBLES AND BARS

Note: In this pattern there are two ways to increase and decrease. You can increase and decrease double crochet stitches to the sides, forming new patterns as stitches are increased and omitting part of pattern as stitches are decreased, or you can increase or decrease the number of double crochet stitches in the panels between the bobbles and bars pattern.

Bobble: *[Yo and pick up a loop around post of dc just made, yo, draw yarn through 2 loops on hook] 5 times, yo and draw yarn through 6 loops on hook.*

Front Post double crochet (FPdc): *Yo, insert hook from front to back to front again around the post of next st, [yo, draw yarn through 2 loops on hook] twice.*

Back Post double crochet (BPdc): *Yo, insert hook from back to front to back again around the post of next st, [yo, draw yarn through 2 loops on hook] twice.*

V-stitch (V-st): *(Dc, ch 1, dc) in same st or sp.*

dc2tog: *Yo, insert hook in next designated st, yo, draw yarn through st, yo, draw yarn through 2 loops on hook] twice, yo, draw yarn through 3 loops on hook.*

Ch 26.

Foundation Row: Dc in 3rd ch from hook (beg ch-2 counts as dc), dc in each ch across, turn. (25 dc)

Row 1: Ch 3 (counts as dc here and throughout), dc in each of the next 3 dc, *ch 1, sk next dc, dc in next dc, bobble over dc just made, ch 1, sk next dc*, dc in each of the next 3 dc, FPdc around the post of next st, sk next dc, V-st in next st, sk next dc, FPdc around the post of next st, dc in each of next 3 dc; rep from * to * once, dc in each of the next 3 dc, dc in top of tch, turn. (2 puff sts; 1 V-st)

Row 2: Ch 3, *dc in each of next 3 dc, dc in next ch-1 sp, dc in next bobble, dc in next ch-1 sp, dc in each of the next 3 dc*, BPdc around the post of next st, V-st in next ch-1 sp, BPdc around the post of next st; rep from * to * once, dc in top of tch, turn.

Rep Rows 1 and 2 for patt, ending with Row 1 of patt to begin increasing.

Increase and Decrease Pattern

Row 1 (inc row): Ch 3, 2 dc in next dc, dc in each of next 2 dc, dc in next ch-1 sp, dc in top of bobble, dc in next ch-1 sp, dc in each of the next 3 dc, BPdc around the post of next st, V-st in next ch-1 sp, BPdc around the post of next st, dc in each of next 3 dc, dc in next ch-1 sp, dc in top of bobble, dc in next ch-1 sp, dc in each of the next 2 dc, 2 dc in next dc, dc in top of tch, turn. (27 dc)

Row 2 (inc row): Ch 3, 2 dc in next dc, *dc in each of the next 3 dc, ch 1, sk next dc, dc next dc, bobble over dc just made, ch 1, sk next dc, dc in each of next 3 dc*, FPdc around the post of next st, V-st in next V-st, sk next dc of V-st, FPdc around the post of next st; rep from * to * once, 2 dc in next dc, dc in top of tch, turn.

Row 3 (inc row): Ch 3, 2 dc in next dc, dc in each of the next 4 dc, *dc in next ch-1 sp, dc in next bobble, dc in next ch-1 sp*, dc in each of the next 3 dc, BPdc around the post of next st, V-st in next ch-1 sp, BPdc around the post of next st, dc in each of next 3 dc; rep from * to * once, dc in each of the next 4 dc, 2 dc in next dc, dc in top of tch, turn.

Row 4 (inc row): Ch 3, 2 dc in next dc, dc in next dc, FPdc around the post of next st, *dc in each of next 3 dc, ch 1, sk next dc, dc in next dc, bobble over dc just made, ch 1, sk next dc, dc in each of the next 3 dc*, FPdc around the post of next st, V-st in next V-st, FPdc around the post of next st; rep from * to * once, FPdc around the post of next st, dc next dc, 2 dc in next dc, dc in top of tch, turn.

Row 5 (inc row): Ch 3, 2 dc in next dc, dc in each of the next 2 dc, BPdc around the post of next st, dc in each of the next 3 dc, *dc in next ch-1 space, dc in next bobble, dc in next ch-1 space*, dc in each of the next 3 dc, 1 BPdc around the post of next st, V-st in next V-st, BPdc around the post of next st 1 dc in each of the next 3 dc; rep from * to * once, dc in each of the next 3 dc, BPdc around the post of next st, dc in each of the next 2 dc, 2 dc in next dc, dc in top of tch, turn.

Row 6 (inc row): Ch 3, 2 dc in next dc, sk next dc, V-st in next dc, sk next dc, FPdc around the post of next st, *dc in each of next 3 dc, ch 1, sk 1 dc, 1 dc next dc, bobble over dc just made, ch 1, sk next dc, dc in each of the next 3 dc, FPdc around the post of next st*, V-st in next V-st, FPdc around the post of next st; rep from * to * once, sk next dc, V-st in next dc, sk next dc, dc in next dc, dc in top of tch, turn.

Rows 7–13: Work even in patt.

Rows 14–19 (dec rows): Ch 3, dc2tog over next 2 sts, work in established patt across to last 3 sts, dc2tog over next 2 sts, dc in top of tch, turn.

Increase and Decrease Method for Bobbles and Bars Pattern

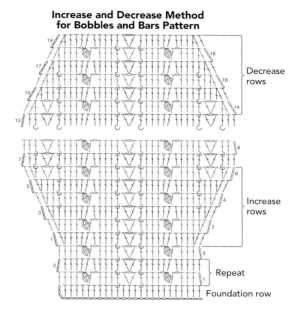

Decrease rows

Increase rows

Repeat

Foundation row

Alternate Increase and Decrease Method for Bobbles and Bars Pattern

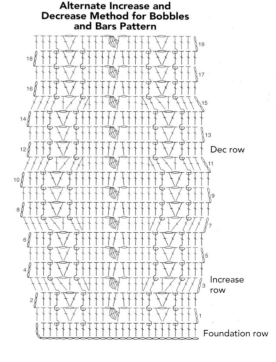

Dec row

Increase row

Foundation row

THE TRIANGLE BODY

If your body type is Triangle, begin your garment following a size that fits your hip measurement, then gradually decrease to fit the waist and chest measurements of a smaller size. Once you have reached your chest measurement, finish the garment following the smaller size instructions.

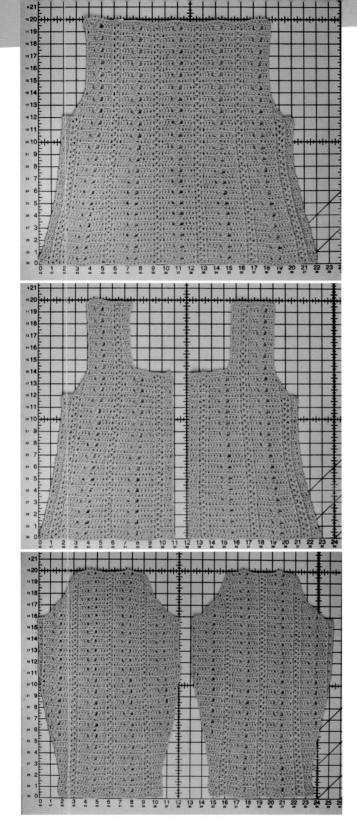

Triangle body type: pieces on blocking board

To customize the style of this sweater, the neckline was lowered by starting the Neck Shaping right after the Armhole Shaping was completed. The Front Borders are worked as for the Rectangle; and Side Puff Scallop Edging (page 101) was added to neck, bottom, and sleeve edges.

THE INVERTED TRIANGLE

If your body type is Inverted Triangle, begin your garment following a size that fits your hip measurement, then gradually increase to the waist and chest measurement of a larger size. Once you have reached your chest measurement, finish the garment following the larger size instructions.

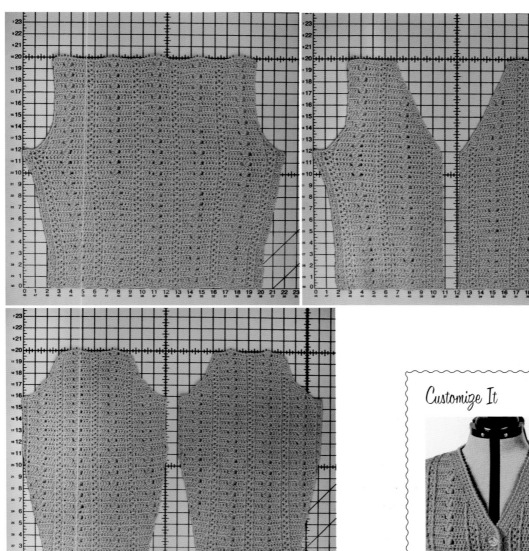

Inverted Triangle body type: pieces on blocking board

Customize It

To customize the style of this sweater, a V-shape neckline was worked (see Shaping Bobbles and Bar, page 34), and a row of reverse single crochet was added to the button band.

THE HOURGLASS

If your body type is Hourglass, begin your garment following a size that fits your hip measurement, then gradually decrease to your waist measurement; work about 2 inches (5 centimeters) even, then gradually increase to your chest measurement. Once you have reached your chest measurement, finish the garment following the size that fits your chest measurement. For this cardigan, the shaping was worked by decreasing and increasing the stitches on either side of the bobble column.

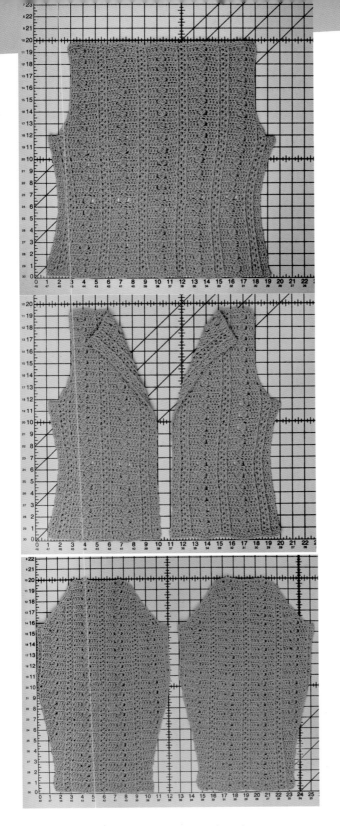

Hourglass body type: pieces on blocking board

Customize It

To customize the style of this sweater, the fronts were completely changed by working as follows:

At the same time as the armhole shaping was started, the FPdcs and BPdcs were gradually reversed. Doing this created a lapel with no disruption to the pattern. The Front was worked all the way to the shoulder with no neck shaping. Then, a collar was made by chaining the same number of stitches as the Back, and working the pattern for 4 inches (10 centimeters).

Finishing: Sew shoulder seams, pin Collar in place with the Right Side of Collar to the Wrong Side of the body, 1 inch (2.5 centimeters) in from each edge. Sew in place, set in Sleeves, sew side seams.

Edgings

Right Front: *Starting at bottom Right Front, Work 1 row sc up to where lapel starts, making 3 button loops evenly spaced, turn. Work 1 Row reverse single crochet omitting button loops. Fasten off.*

Left Front: *Starting at lapel, work 1 row sc, then 1 row reverse sc.*

Lapel and Collar: *Starting at beginning of lapel on Left Front, work 1 row sc all around Lapels and Collar, then 1 row reverse sc. Fasten off.*

Cluster Cardigan

Cluster stitches are usually quite heavy, so when using them for a garment, I like to use a crochet hook that is one size larger than the recommended hook. This loosens the stitch a little and gives the resulting fabric softer drape.

SKILL LEVEL
INTERMEDIATE

CLASSIC RECTANGLE

Yarn: Light (3)

Shown: LB Collection Superwash Merino, 100% Superwash Merino Wool, 306 yds/280 m, 3.5 oz/100 g, 6 (6, 7, 8) skeins #107 Sky

Hooks: G/6 (4 mm) and H/8 (5 mm) or sizes to obtain gauge

Gauge: With larger hook, 6 clusters = 4" (10 cm); 12 rows in patt = 4" (10 cm).

Notions

Yarn needle

Five ¾" (19mm) buttons

Sewing needle and matching sewing thread

Sizes: Small (Medium, Large, X large)

Finished Bust: 32 (36, 40, 44)" (81.5 [91.5, 101.5, 112] cm)]

Cluster Stitch Pattern

Ch a multiple of 3 plus 2.

Row 1: (Sc, hdc, dc) in 2nd ch from hook (cluster made), sk next 2 ch, *(sc, hdc, dc) in next ch, sk 2 chs, rep from * across, sc in last ch, turn.

Row 2: Ch 2, (sc, hdc, dc) in first sc, *sk next 2 sts, (sc, hdc, dc) in next sc, rep from * across ending with sc in last sc, turn.

Rep Row 2 for patt.

Reduced sample of pattern

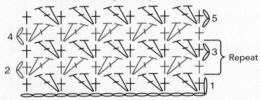

BACK

With H/8 (5 mm) hook, ch 71 (80, 89, 98).

Row 1 (RS): (Sc, hdc, dc) in 2nd ch from hook (cluster made), sk next 2 ch, *(sc, hdc, dc) in next ch, sk 2 chs, rep from * across, sc in last ch, turn. (23 [26, 29, 32] clusters)

Row 2: Ch 2, (sc, hdc, dc) in first sc, *sk next 2 sts, (sc, hdc, dc) in next sc, rep from * across, ending with sc in top of tch, turn.

Rep Row 2 for patt until Back measures 13½ (14, 14½, 15)" (34.5 [35.5, 37, 38] cm) from beg.

Shape Armholes

Row 1: Sl st in each of first 7 sts, work in patt as established across to last 9 sts, sk next 2 sts, sc in next sc, turn, leaving rem sts unworked. (19 [22, 25, 28] clusters)

Row 2 (dec row): Ch 1, (sc, hdc) in first sc, work in patt across to last 6 sts, sk next 2 sts, (sc, hdc) in next sc, sk next 2 sts, sc in last sc, turn.

Row 3 (dec row): Ch 1, sc in first sc, sk next hdc, work in patt across to last 5 sts, sk next 2 sts, sc in next sc, sk next hdc, sc in last sc, turn.

Row 4 (dec row): Ch 1, sk in first sc, work in patt across to last 4 sts, sk next 3 sts, sc in last sc, turn. (17 [20, 23, 26] clusters)

Work even until armhole measures 7½ (8, 8½, 9)" (19 [20.5, 21.5, 23] cm) from beg. Fasten off.

LEFT FRONT

With H/8 (5 mm) hook, ch 38 (41, 47, 50).

Work same as back on 12 (13, 15, 16) clusters to Shape Armhole, ending at armhole edge.

Shape Armhole

Row 1: Sl st in each of first 7 sts, work in patt as established across, turn. (10 [11, 13, 14] clusters)

Row 2: Work in patt across, turn.

Row 3 (dec row): Ch 2, (sc, hdc) in first sc, work in patt across, turn.

Row 4 (dec row): Work in patt across to last 5 sts, sk next 2 sts, sc in next sc, sk next hdc, sc in last sc, turn.

Row 5 (dec row): Ch 2, sc in first sc, work in patt across, turn. (9 [10, 12, 13] clusters).

Work even in patt until armhole measures 3½ (4, 4½, 5)" (9 [10, 11.5, 12.5] cm) from beg, ending at armhole edge.

Shape Neck

Next Row: Work in patt across first 5 (5, 6, 6) clusters, sc in next sc, turn, leaving rem sts unworked. (5 [5, 6, 6] clusters)

Work even in patt as established until Left Front measures same as Back to shoulder. Fasten off.

RIGHT FRONT

Work same as Left Front to Shape Armhole.

Shape Armhole

Row 1: Work in patt across to last 9 sts, sk next 2 sts, sc in next sc, turn, leaving rem sts unworked.

Row 2 (dec row): Ch 2, (sc, hdc) in first sc, work in patt across, turn.

Row 3 (dec row): Work in patt across to last 5 sts, sk next 2 sts, sc in next sc, sk next hdc, sc in last sc, turn.

Row 4 (dec row): Ch 2, sc in first sc, work in patt across, turn. (9 [10, 12, 13] clusters)

Work even in patt until armhole measures 3½ (4, 4½, 5)" (9 [10, 11.5, 12.5] cm) from beg, ending at front edge.

Shape Neck

Sl st in each of first 13 (16, 19, 22) sts, ch 2, work in patt as established across rem 5 (5, 6, 6) clusters, turn.

Work even in patt as established until Right Front measures same as Back to shoulder. Fasten off.

SLEEVE (MAKE TWO)

With H/8 (5 mm) hook, ch 38 (41, 44, 47).

Work even in patt same as Back on 12 (13, 14, 15) Cl until Sleeve measures 3" (7.5 cm) from beg.

Next Row (inc row): Ch 4, (sc, hdc, dc) in first sc, *sk next 2 ch, (sc, hdc, dc) in next ch; rep from * across, ending with (sc, hdc, dc) in last ch, turn. (1 cluster inc)

Next Row (inc row): Ch 2, (sc, hdc, dc) in first dc, *sk next 2 ch, (sc, hdc, dc) in next ch; rep from * across, ending with (sc, hdc, dc) in last sc, sc in beg ch-4, turn. (1 cluster inc)

Work even for 2" (5 cm).

Work 2 inc rows every 2" (5 cm) 3 more times. (20 [21, 22, 23] clusters at end of last 2 inc rows).

Work even in patt as established until Sleeve measures 16 (16 1/2, 17, 17½)" (40.5 [42, 43, 44.5] cm) from beg.

Shape Cap

Row 1: Sl st in each of first 7 sts, work in patt as established across to last 9 sts, sk next 2 sts, sc in next sc, turn, leaving rem sts unworked. (16 [17, 18, 19] clusters)

Dec 1 cluster at beg of every row 12 (14, 16, 18) times. Fasten Off. (See Shaping Cluster Stitch page 51). (4 [3, 2, 1] clusters at end of last row)

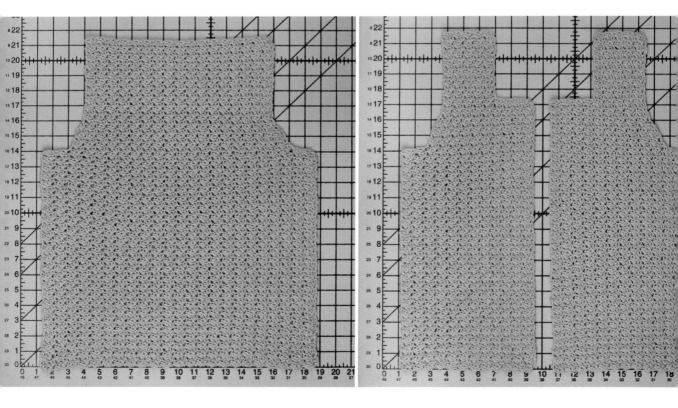

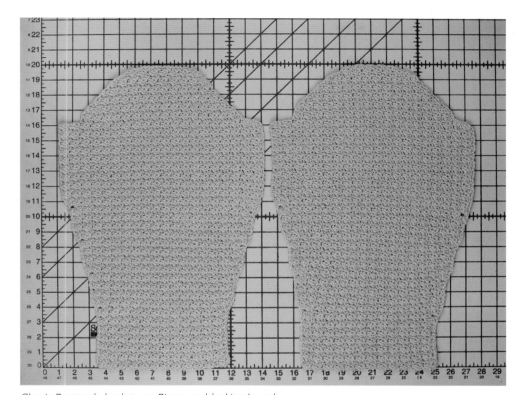

Classic Rectangle body type: Pieces on blocking board

ASSEMBLY

Sew shoulder seams. Mark center of Sleeve Cap. Matching center of sleeve cap to shoulder seam and matching bound off armhole edges, pin in place, easing cap around shoulder. Sew in place. Sew underarm seams.

Neck and Front Border

Row 1: With RS facing and G/6 (4 mm) hook, join yarn with sl st in bottom Right Front corner, ch 1, work 64 (66, 68, 70) sc evenly spaced across to top corner of Right Front, work 3 sc in corner, work 32 (34, 36, 38) sc evenly spaced across to shoulder seam, sc in each st across back neck edge to shoulder seam, work 32 (34, 36, 38) sc evenly spaced across to top of Left Front corner, work 3 sc in corner, work 64 (66, 68, 70) sc evenly spaced across to bottom Left Front corner, turn.

Row 2: Ch 1, sc in each sc across to next corner, 3 sc in corner st, sk 1 st, sc in each st across to 1 st before next corner st, sk 1 st, 3 sc in corner st, sc in each st across to bottom corner, turn.

Row 3 (buttonhole row): Ch 1, sc in each of first 6 (8, 10 12) sc, [ch 3, sk next 2 sts, sc in each of next 9 sc] 4 times, ch 3, sk next 2 sts, sc in each sc across to next corner st, 3 sc in corner st, sk 1 st, sc in each st across to 1 st before next corner st, sk 1 st, 3 sc in corner st, sc in each st across to bottom corner, turn.

Row 4: Ch 1, sc in each st across to next corner st, 3 sc in corner st, sk 1 st, sc in each st across to 1 st before corner st, sk 1 st, 3 sc in corner, [sc in each st across to next ch-3 sp, 2 sc in next ch-3 space] 5 times, sc in each across to next corner, turn.

Row 5: Rep Row 2, do not turn. Fasten off.

FINISHING

With sewing needle and thread, sew buttons to Left Front opposite buttonholes.

Blocking: Lay garment on a padded surface and sprinkle with water. Pat into shape. Pin out to measurements using rustproof pins. Allow to dry.

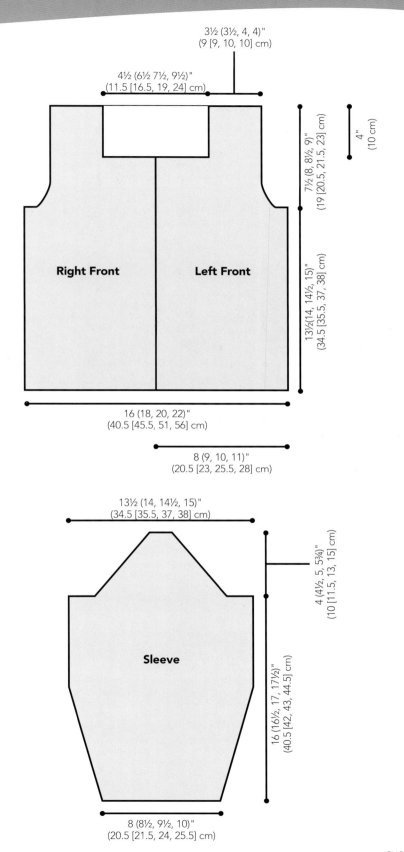

3½ (3½, 4, 4)"
(9 [9, 10, 10] cm)

4½ (6½ 7½, 9½)"
(11.5 [16.5, 19, 24] cm)

4"
(10 cm)

7½ (8, 8½, 9)"
(19 [20.5, 21.5, 23] cm)

Right Front

Left Front

13½(14, 14½, 15)"
(34.5 [35.5, 37, 38] cm)

16 (18, 20, 22)"
(40.5 [45.5, 51, 56] cm)

8 (9, 10, 11)"
(20.5 [23, 25.5, 28] cm)

13½ (14, 14½, 15)"
(34.5 [35.5, 37, 38] cm)

4 (4½, 5, 5¾)"
(10 [11.5, 13, 15] cm)

Sleeve

16 (16½, 17, 17½)"
(40.5 [42, 43, 44.5] cm)

8 (8½, 9½, 10)"
(20.5 [21.5, 24, 25.5] cm)

Customizing the Fit

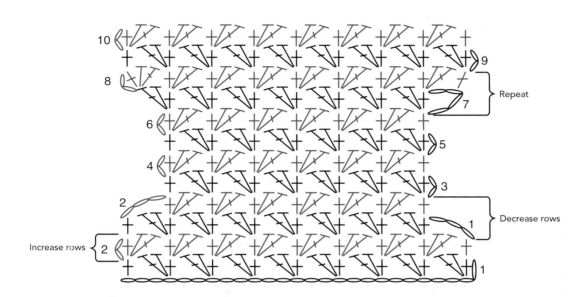

SHAPING CLUSTER STITCH

Ch a multiple of 3 plus 2.

Row 1: (Sc, hdc, dc) in 2nd ch from hook, *sk next 2 ch, (sc, hdc, dc) in next ch; rep from * across to last 3 ch, sk next 2 ch, sc in last ch, turn.

Row 2: Ch 2, (sc, hdc, dc) in first sc, *sk next 2 sts, (sc, hdc, dc) in next sc; rep from * across to last 3 sts, sk next 2 sts, sc in last sc, turn.

Rep Row 2 for patt.

INCREASE AND DECREASE PATTERN

Row 1 (dec row): Ch 3, sk first 3 sts, (sc, hdc, dc) in next sc, sk next 2 sts; rep from * across, ending with sc in last sc, turn. (1 cluster dec)

Row 2 (dec row): Ch 3, sk first 3 sts, (sc, hdc, dc) in next sc, sk next 2 sts; rep from * across, ending with sc in last sc, turn. (1 cluster dec)

Rows 3–6: Work even in patt.

Row 7 (inc row): Ch 4, (sc, hdc, dc) in first sc, *sk next 2 ch, (sc, hdc, dc) in next ch; rep from * across, ending with (sc, hdc, dc) in last ch, turn. (1 cluster inc)

Row 8: Ch 2, (sc, hdc, dc) in first dc, *sk next 2 ch, (sc, hdc, dc) in next ch; rep from * across, ending with (sc, hdc, dc) in last sc, sc in beg ch-4, turn. (1 cluster inc)

Rows 9–10: Work even in patt.

THE TRIANGLE BODY

If your body type is Triangle, begin your garment following a size that fits your hip measurement, then gradually decrease to fit the waist and chest measurements of a smaller size. Once you have reached your chest measurement, finish the garment following the smaller size instructions.

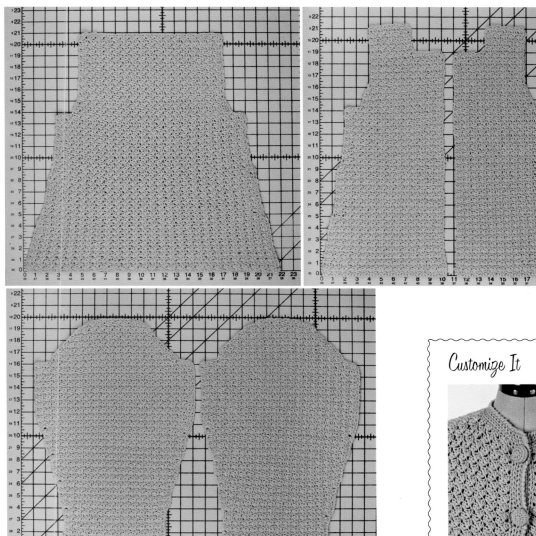

Triangle body type: pieces on blocking board

Customize It

To customize the style of this sweater, 1 row of reverse single crochet was added to the edgings and covered buttons (page 107) were used.

THE INVERTED TRIANGLE

If your body type is Inverted Triangle, begin your garment following a size that fits your hip measurement, then gradually increase to the waist and chest measurement of a larger size. Once you have reached your chest measurement, finish the garment following the larger size instructions.

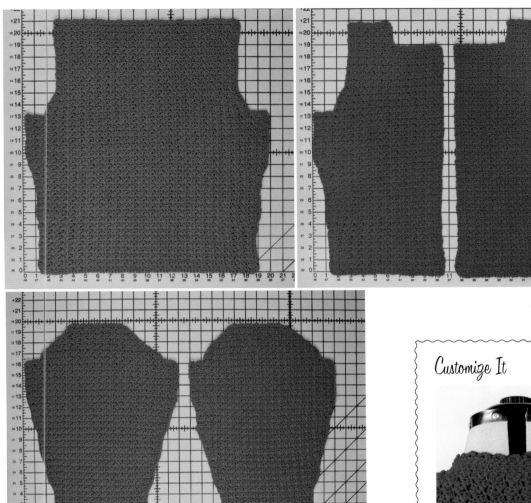

Inverted Triangle body type: pieces on blocking board

Customize It

To customize the style of this sweater, the final buttonhole was placed 3 inches (7.5 centimeters) below the neck edge, allowing the front to fold back and form a small lapel. The Ruffle edging (page 103) was also added.

THE HOURGLASS

If your body type is Hourglass, begin your garment following a size that fits your hip measurement, then gradually decrease to your waist measurement, work about 2 inches (5 centimeters) even, then gradually increase to your chest measurement. Once you have reached your chest measurement, finish the garment following the size that fits your chest measurement.

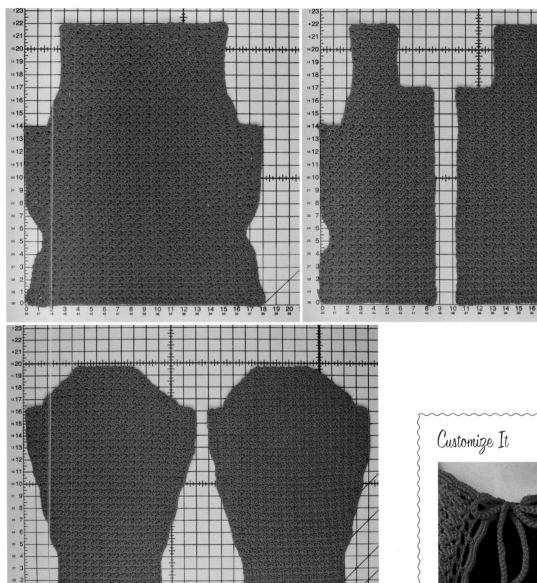

Hourglass body type: pieces on blocking board

Customize It

To customize the style of this sweater, the Simple Scallop (page 101), was worked and a chain tie was made at the neck for fastening.

Rose Petal Vine Cardigan

There are many open, lacy crochet stitches that require a large multiple to complete the pattern. Rose Petal Vine is one of these patterns. The large multiple makes customizing the fit of these garment patterns quite difficult. I find that changing the hook size, rather than increasing or decreasing stitches, works quite well and is much easier to manage.

SKILL LEVEL
INTERMEDIATE

CLASSIC RECTANGLE

Yarn: Light (3)

Shown: LB Collection Superwash Merino, 100% Superwash Merino Wool, 306 yds/280 m, 3.5 oz/100 g, 6 (6, 7, 8) skeins #139 Peony

Hooks: G/6 (4 mm), H/8 (5 mm), I/9 (5.5 mm), and J/10 (6 mm) or sizes to obtain gauge

Gauge: To check your gauge, using H/8 (5 mm) hook, ch 23, change to G/6 (4 mm) hook work in patt for 10 rows. Piece should measure 4 x 4" (10 x 10 cm).

Notions

Yarn needle

Three ½" (12mm) buttons

Sewing needle and matching sewing thread

Sizes: Small (Medium, Large, X large)

Finished Bust: 32 (36, 40, 44)" (81 [91.5, 101.5, 111.5] cm)

Special Stitches

Cluster (CL): [Yo, pick up a loop in designated st, yo, draw yarn through 2 loops on hook] 3 times, yo, draw yarn through all 4 loops on hook.

Reduced Sample of Pattern

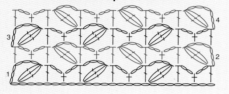

Note: Rather than increasing or decreasing stitches in this patt, different size hooks are used for shaping Sleeves.

ROSE PETAL VINE PATTERN

Ch a multiple of 8 plus 7.

Row 1 (RS): CL in 7th ch from hook, sk next 3 ch, 1 dc in next ch, *ch 2, sk next ch, sc in next ch, ch 2, sk next ch**, [dc, ch 3, CL] in next ch, sk next 3 ch, dc in next ch, rep from * across, ending last rep at **, dc in last ch, turn.

Row 2: Ch 6 (counts as dc, ch 3), CL in first dc, *sk next 2 ch-2 sps, dc in next dc, ch 2, sc in next ch-3 sp, ch 2**, [dc, ch 3, CL] in next dc, rep from * across, ending last rep at **, dc in 3rd ch of ch-6 tch, turn.

Rep Row 2 for patt.

BACK

With H/8 (5 mm) hook, ch 71 (79, 87, 95).

Change to G/6 (4 mm) hook and work patt until piece measures 12½ (13, 13½, 14)" (31.5 [33, 34.5, 35.5] cm) from beg. (8 [9, 10, 12] patt reps)

Shape Armholes

Row 1: Ch 1, sl st in first sp, sl st in next sc, sl st in next sp, sl st in next dc, ch 5 (counts as dc, ch 2 here and throughout), sc in next ch-3 sp, ch 2, *(dc, ch 3, CL) in next dc, dc in next dc**, ch 2, sc in next ch-3 sp, ch 2, rep from * across, ending last rep at **, turn, leaving rem sts unworked. (7 [8, 9, 10] patt reps)

Work even in patt until armhole measures 7½ (8, 8½, 9)" (19 [20.5, 21.5, 23] cm) from beg. Fasten off.

FIRST FRONT

With H/8 (5 mm) hook, ch 39 (43, 47, 51).

Row 1: Change to G/6 (4 mm) hook, CL in 7th ch from hook, sk next 3 ch, dc in next ch, *ch 2, sk next ch, sc in next ch, ch 2, sk next ch**, (dc, ch 3, CL) in next ch, sk next 3 ch*, dc in next ch, rep from * across, ending last rep at * (**, *, **), dc in 3rd ch of beg ch, turn. (4 [4½, 5, 5½] reps)

Shape Armhole

SIZES S AND L ONLY

Row 1: Ch 1, sl st in each st and sp across to next dc, ch 5 (counts as dc, ch 2), sc in next ch-3 sp, ch 2, *(dc, ch 3, CL) in next dc, dc in next dc, ch 2, sc in next ch-3 sp, ch 2, rep from * across, dc in 3rd ch of beg ch-6, turn. (3½ [4½] reps)

Row 2: Ch 6, CL in first dc, dc in next dc, *ch 2, sc in next ch-3 sp, ch 2, (dc, ch 3 CL) in next dc, dc in next dc, rep from * across, ending with last dc in 3rd ch of beg ch-5, turn. (3½ [4½] reps)

SIZES M AND XL ONLY

Row 1: Ch 1, sl st in each st and sp across to next dc, ch 6, CL in first dc, dc in next dc, *ch 2, sc in next ch-3 sp, ch 2**, (dc, ch 3, CL) in next dc, dc in next dc, rep from * across, ending last rep at **, dc in 3rd ch of beg ch-6, turn. (4 [5] reps)

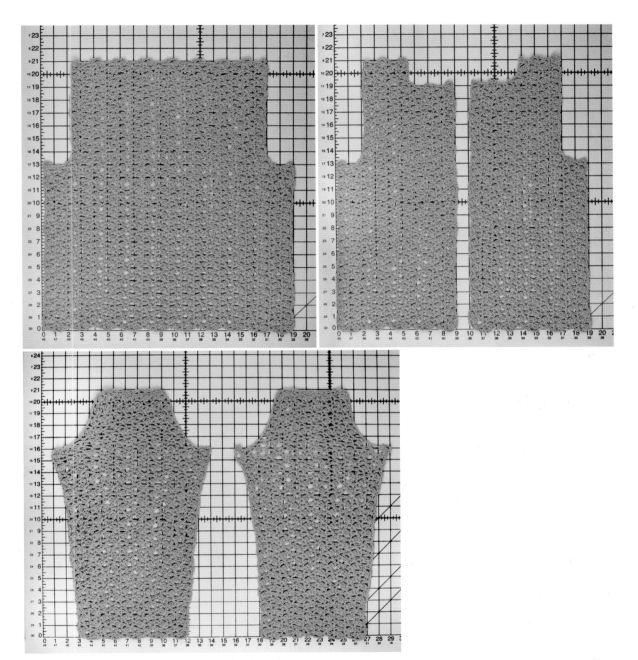

Classic Rectangle body type: pieces on blocking board

ALL SIZES

Work even in established patt until armhole measures 5 (5½, 6, 6½)" (12.5 [14, 15, 16.5] cm) from beg, ending at armhole edge.

Shape Neck

Row 1: Work even in patt as established across first 2 (2, 2½, 2½) patt reps ending with dc in 5th (5th, 6th, 6th) dc, turn, leaving rep sts unworked. (2 [2, 2½, 2½] reps)

Work even in established patt until Front measures same as Back to shoulder. Fasten off.

SECOND FRONT

Work same as First Front to Armhole Shaping.

Armhole Shaping

Row 1: Work in established patt across row to within last 2 ch-2 sps, turn leaving rem sts unworked. (3½ [4, 4½, 5] reps)

Work even in established patt until armhole measures 5 (5½, 6, 6½)" (12.5 [14, 15, 16.5] cm) from beg, ending at front edge.

Shape Neck

Row 1: Sl st across until 2 (2, 2½, 2½) patt reps remain, ch 5 (5, 6, 6), work in established patt across, turn.

Work even in established patt until Front measures same as Back to shoulder. Fasten off.

SLEEVE (MAKE 2)

Using G/6 (4 mm) hook, ch 47 (55, 63, 71).

Work in patt same as back until Sleeve measures 3" (7.5 cm) from beg. (5 [6, 7, 8] reps). Change to H/8 (5 mm) hook. Work even in patt until Sleeve measures 9" (23 cm) from beg. Change to I/9 (5,5 mm) hook. Work even in patt until Sleeve measures 16 (16½, 17, 17½)" (40.5 [42, 43, 44.5] cm) from beg.

Shape Cap

Row 1: With I/9 (5.5 mm) hook, ch 1, sl st in first sp, sl st in next sc, sl st in next sp, sl st in next dc, ch 5 (counts as dc, ch 2 here and throughout), sc in next ch-3 sp, ch 2, *(dc, ch 3 CL) in next dc, dc in next dc**, ch 2, sc in next ch-3 sp, ch 2, rep from * across, ending last rep at **, turn, leaving rem sts unworked. (4 [5, 6, 7] patt reps) Work even for 3 (4, 5, 6) more rows. Change to H/8 (5 mm) hook. Work even for 2 (3, 4, 5) more rows. Change to G/6 (4 mm) hook. Work even for 2 more rows.

Next Row: Ch 1, sc in first dc, ch 1, *sc in next ch-3 sp, ch 1, sc in next ch-2 sp, ch 1, sc in next ch-2 sp, ch 1, rep from * across, ending with sc in 3rd ch of beg ch-3.

Next Row: Ch 1, skipping all ch-1 sps, work sc in each sc across, ending with sc in last sc. Fasten off.

ASSEMBLY

Sew shoulder seams. Mark center of Sleeve Cap. Matching center of sleeve cap to shoulder seam and matching bound off armhole edges, pin in place, easing cap around shoulder. Sew in place. Sew underarm seams.

Neck and Front Border

Row 1: With RS facing and G/6 (4 mm) hook, join yarn with sl st in bottom Right Front corner, ch 1, work 73 (75, 77, 79) sc evenly spaced across to top corner of Right Front, work 3 sc in corner, work 22 (26, 26, 30) sc evenly spaced across to shoulder seam, sc evenly across back neck edge to left shoulder seam, work 22 (26, 26, 30) sc evenly spaced across to top of Left Front corner, work 3 sc in corner, work 73 (75, 77, 79) sc evenly spaced across to bottom corner of left front, turn.

Row 2: Ch 1, sc in each sc across to next corner, 3 sc in corner st, sk 1 st, sc in each st across to 1 st before next corner st, sk 1 st, 3 sc in corner st, sc in each st across to bottom corner, turn.

Row 3 (buttonhole row): Ch 1, sc in each of first 17 (20, 23, 26) sc, [ch 2, sk next 2 sts, sc in each of next 5 sc] twice, ch 2, sk next 2 sts, sc in each sc across to next corner st, 3 sc in corner st, sk 1 st, sc in each st across to 1 st before next corner st, sk 1 st, 3 sc in corner st, sc in each st across to bottom corner, turn.

Row 4: Ch 1, sc in each st across to next corner st, 3 sc in corner st, sk 1 st, sc in each st across to 1 st before corner st, sk 1 st, 3 sc in corner, [sc in each st across to next ch-2 sp, 2 sc in next ch-2 space] 3 times, sc in each across to next corner, turn.

Row 5: Rep Row 2, do not turn.

Row 6: Ch 1, working from left to right, reverse sc in each st across. Fasten off.

FINISHING

With sewing needle and thread, sew buttons to Left Front opposite buttonholes.

Blocking: Lay garment on a padded surface and sprinkle with water. Pat into shape. Pin out to measurements using rustproof pins. Allow to dry.

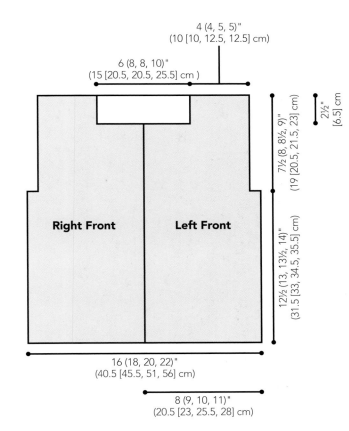

4 (4, 5, 5)"
(10 [10, 12.5, 12.5] cm)

6 (8, 8, 10)"
(15 [20.5, 20.5, 25.5] cm)

2½"
[6.5] cm

7½ (8, 8½, 9)"
(19 [20.5, 21.5, 23] cm)

Right Front

Left Front

12½ (13, 13½, 14)"
(31.5 [33, 34.5, 35.5] cm)

16 (18, 20, 22)"
(40.5 [45.5, 51, 56] cm)

8 (9, 10, 11)"
(20.5 [23, 25.5, 28] cm)

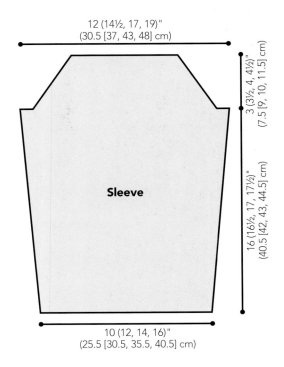

12 (14½, 17, 19)"
(30.5 [37, 43, 48] cm)

3 (3½, 4, 4½)"
(7.5 [9, 10, 11.5] cm)

Sleeve

16 (16½, 17, 17½)"
(40.5 [42, 43, 44.5] cm)

10 (12, 14, 16)"
(25.5 [30.5, 35.5, 40.5] cm)

Customizing the Fit

SHAPING ROSE PETAL VINES

It is difficult to increase and decrease in this pattern stitch. Therefore, a different method of shaping is used for this project. The measurements are altered by using different hook sizes to change the gauge while keeping the stitch counts the same. Because you begin the sweater at the bottom, select the sweater size that fits your hip measurement. After working gauge swatches to find the correct hook size, begin with that hook. Then change hook sizes up or down as necessary to alter the gauge, but continue to follow the same pattern size instructions. Depending on how radically your measurements differ from the pattern schematics, you may have to change hook sizes several times. If done gradually, one hook size at a time, the change in the size of the stitches is less noticeable.

THE TRIANGLE BODY

If your body type is triangle, begin your garment following a size that fits your hip measurement, using the hook that provides the designated gauge. Then switch to a smaller hook as you approach the waist. Change to a smaller hook(s) again as you approach and work through the chest to the shoulders. Measure frequently to check your adjustments.

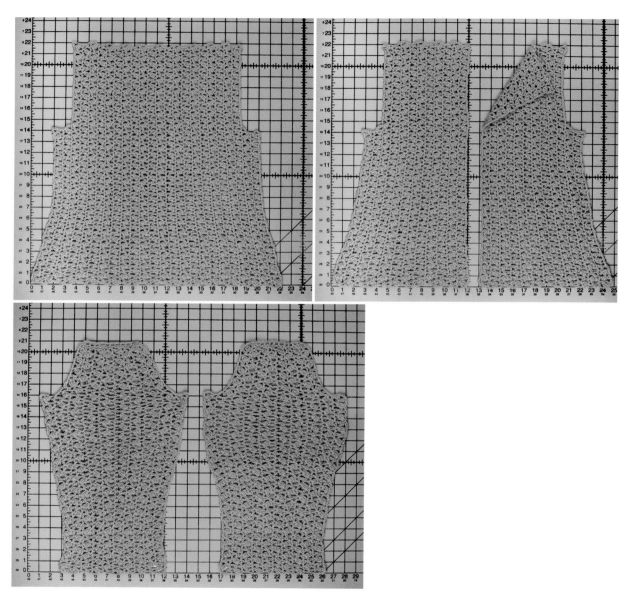

Triangle body type: pieces on blocking board

Customize It

To customize the style of this sweater, the neck shaping is eliminated and the fronts are worked straight up to neckline. Sew the shoulder seams. Then, starting at Bottom Right Front, work as follows:

Work 1 row sc all around edge to Bottom Left Front, turn, ch 1, work 1 row sc all around to Right Front at about armhole height, [chain 10 (for a button loop), 1 sc in each of next 10 sc] twice, ch 10, continue sc to bottom of Right Front, fasten off.

Fold the Fronts back to form a V-neck and tack in place.

Embellish with appliques sewn onto folded back edges and around back of neck. The sample shows two 5 Petal Flowers (page 90), four Fanciful Fans (page 91), and three Open Leaf Motifs (page 92).

THE INVERTED TRIANGLE

If your body type is Inverted Triangle, begin your garment following a size that fits your hip measurement, using the hook that provides the designated gauge. Then switch to a larger hook as you approach the waist. Change to a larger hook(s) again as you approach and work through the chest to the shoulders. Measure frequently to check your adjustments.

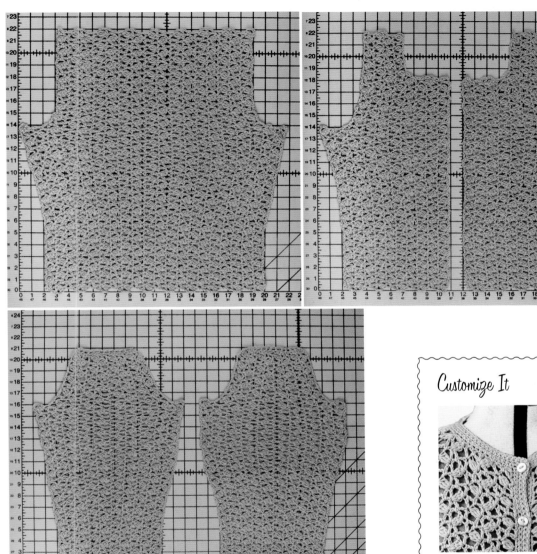

Inverted Triangle body type: pieces on blocking board

THE HOURGLASS

If your body type is Hourglass, begin your garment following a size that fits your hip measurement, using the hook that provides the designated gauge. Then switch to a smaller hook as you approach and work through the waist. Change back to the original hook again as you approach and work through the chest to the shoulders. Measure frequently to check your adjustments.

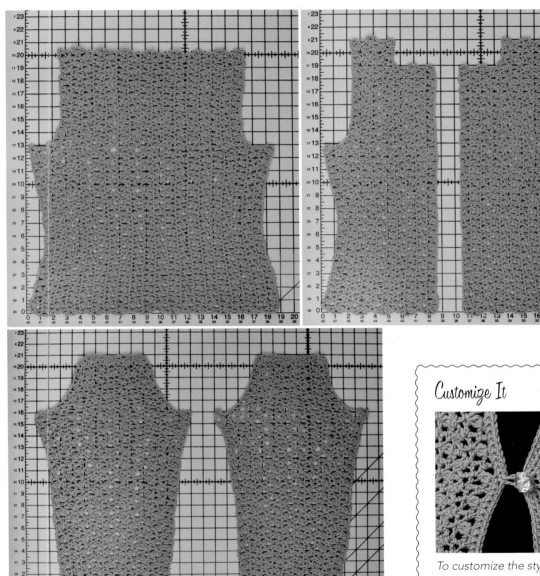

Hourglass body type: pieces on blocking board

Customize It

To customize the style of this sweater, three rows of single crochet are worked all around the Front and Neck Edges, with a single button loop at the waistline for fastening.

Finish Like a Pro

The quality of the finishing work in any project is essential to the success of that project. There are various ways to sew seams, sew on buttons, finish off an edge, and block your project. In this section, methods for each of these finishing steps are discussed. Learning these techniques and knowing when to use them will help you finish your crocheted garments like a pro.

Good Habits

Let's begin with a few important practices that will help you crochet professional-looking garments.

TEST YOUR GAUGE

Making a gauge swatch before starting your project is so important that failing to do it pretty much guarantees failure of the project.

In order to crochet a garment that looks like the project shown, and matches the finished measurements given in the instructions, it is important to choose a yarn in the weight specified in the pattern. This is the first requirement to getting the proper gauge for your project. Gauge refers to the number of stitches and the number of rows in a given width and length, usually over 4" (10 cm) of crocheted fabric. The hook size recommended is the size an average crocheter would use to get the correct gauge. We can't all be average. Some of us crochet tighter, some looser.

Before beginning to crochet a project, it is very important to take the time to check your gauge. Start by making a chain a little over 4" (10 cm) long; and work the pattern stitch, using the yarn and hook called for in the instructions, until you have a square approximately 4" (10 cm). Place a pin on one side of the work and place another pin 4" (10 cm) over. Count the stitches between the pins. If you have more stitches to the inch than the instructions call for, your work is too tight: try another swatch using a larger hook. If you have fewer stitches to the inch than the instructions call for, your work is too loose; try using a smaller hook. It is better to change hook size to get the proper gauge, rather than trying to work tighter or looser, because your gauge will be more consistent.

If you substitute a different yarn with similar weight for any project, it is not enough to simply compare the gauge on the yarn ball band to that of the project.

Consider the ball band information to be a starting point and continue to crochet gauge swatches and change hook sizes until you are working at the exact gauge required in the pattern.

THE ALL-IMPORTANT FOUNDATION CHAIN

Take another look at your gauge swatch. The foundation chain should lie flat and move with the same amount of stretch as rest of the swatch. If it is tighter than the rest of your swatch, which is a common problem, the beginning rows will draw in and distort the garment. If it is too tight, the garment won't fit well, and the foundation chain may snap and ravel at some point. In this case, make the foundation chain with a larger hook. If the foundation chain waves because it is too loose, the edge of the garment will look sloppy. In this case, crochet it with a smaller hook. Once you have made a foundation chain you are happy with, switch back to the hook that works for the required gauge.

BECOME A ROW COUNTER

Measuring carefully as you work is important, and learning to count rows is another way to contribute to the success of your finished piece. For example, perhaps your instructions tell you to work until the piece measures 11" (28 cm) from the bottom to the armhole, shape the armhole, then work 7½"(19 cm) to the shoulder, shape shoulder, and fasten off. When you crochet the fronts, rather than relying on measuring alone, crochet the same number of rows for each section. In this way, when you are ready to sew the pieces together, they will match up row for row and the seams will lie flat and even. Counting rows ensures that the sleeves will be the same length; and the fronts will match perfectly.

Seams

There are several different ways to sew seams. Which method to use is sometimes a matter of preference; sometimes one way is better for a certain stitch. You may even use two different methods on the same garment: one to create side seams that lie flat, and a sturdier stitch for setting in a sleeve or sewing a shoulder seam. Pinning your pieces together before starting to sew helps keep them even as you work.

The order in which the seams are sewn is also important. For set-in or drop shoulder sleeves, sew the shoulder seams first. Then sew in the sleeves, and finish by sewing the underarm sleeve and side seams. For a garment with raglan sleeves or saddle shoulders, there are no shoulder seams; sew sleeves above the armholes to the garment fronts and backs. The top of the sleeve becomes part of the neckline.

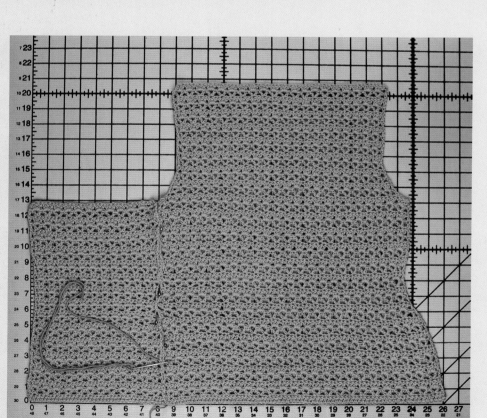

The woven seam works well for side seams, and was used for the Double Crochet Lace Cardigan.

Wrong side

Right side

WOVEN SEAM

Use this method for a very flat seam. When done properly, you will not even see your stitches. Hold the pieces to be seamed side by side and, working from the wrong side, insert the needle from front to back through one loop only, draw the yarn through and progress to the next stitch, bring needle through (not over) from back to front, and proceed in this manner until the seam is completed. If you draw the yarn through the top loop only, a decorative ridge will be left on the right side of work. If you draw through bottom loops, the ridge of the seam will be on the inside (wrong side) of the work.

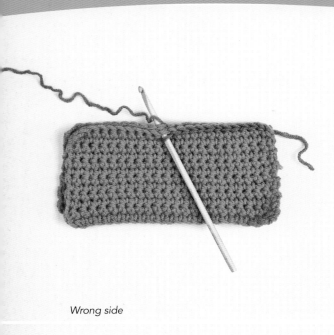

Wrong side

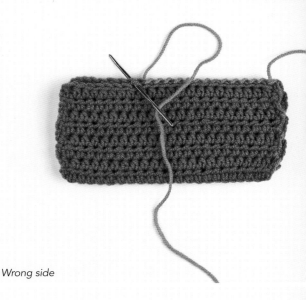

Wrong side

Right side

Right side

SLIP STITCH SEAM

The slip-stitch join is a favorite of many because it is quick and easy to do. Work loosely to avoid puckering seams. Place the right sides together, draw up a loop through both layers of fabric, one stitch in from the edge of the seam, insert the hook in next the stitch, and draw up a loop; continue in this manner until seam is completed.

OVERCAST SEAM

The overcast seam, also called whipstitch seam, works best for sewing straight edges together. Holding the right sides together, insert the needle from front to back through the inside loops, bring the yarn through and around, and repeat.

Wrong side

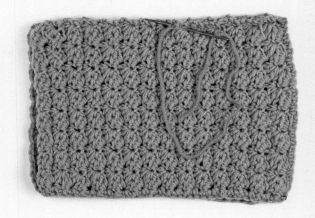

Wrong side

Right side

Right side

SINGLE CROCHET SEAM

The single crochet seam creates a decorative ridge, so you might want to use it for prominent side seams or for joining a trim to a garment edge. Holding the pieces with the wrong sides together, work single crochet through the whole stitch on both edges to be joined.

BACKSTITCH SEAM

The backstitch seam works well for joining a set-in sleeve. This method does have some internal bulk, but if done properly, it is strong and helps shape the seam cap nicely. The backstitch method is also a good choice for joining shaped edges. This seam is worked with the right sides together.

Attaching Sleeves

Take care when sewing the sleeves to your garment. The sleeves should fit the armhole smoothly, without puckering, and hang straight, centered in the armhole.

To attach sleeves, first sew the shoulder seams. Then mark the center of the sleeve cap and pin the sleeve in place, matching the center of the cap to the shoulder seam. Ease the sleeve to fit, pinning the edges together from the center to the underarms. Sew the sleeves in place, using the backstitch seam for set-in sleeves (where the seam is at the crown of the shoulder). Use one of the more invisible, flat seaming methods for sewing drop shoulder sleeves in place.

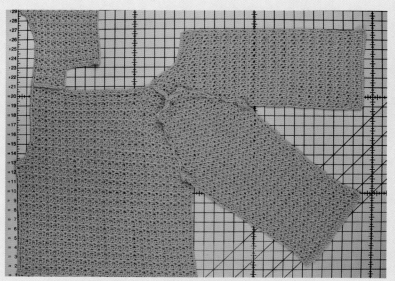

Sleeve pinned in place, wrong sides together, ready to sew.

Backstitch is a sturdy seam that helps the armhole hold its shape.

Collars and Neckbands

Most collars on crocheted items are made separately and sewn on, or picked up and worked along the front, neck and back edges, usually on a smaller hook than the body of the garment. This is necessary for good fit in the neck area, as we usually start shaping the neck about 2 to 3 inches (5 to 7.5 centimeters) below the back of neck, making a curve to fit the neck shape.

Front Borders

The front borders, or button/buttonhole bands, on a cardigan are a visual focal point, so it is crucial that they look flawless. The best way to achieve this is to ensure that the stitches for these bands are picked up evenly along the row-ends of the front edges. Because crochet stitches are not "square", meaning they are not the same height as width, this can be one of the hardest things to do. Use the following method as a guide: Divide the front into four sections, placing pins to mark each quarter. Count the rows in each section to be sure they are equal, divide the designated number of stitches by four, then pick up the appropriate number of stitches evenly between the pins.

The general rule of thumb is to pick up one stitch in every other row for single crochet, or one stitch in every row for double crochet. Therefore, if you have 20 rows of single crochet, you'll pick up 10 stitches along the row-ends. If you have 20 rows of double crochet, you will pick up 20 stitches. These guidelines work for most people, but not all. Your work must lie flat, and sometimes you will have to experiment to judge how to proceed. If your edges are rippling, like a ruffle, you are picking up too many stitches; if they are pulling in, you are picking up too few stitches. In either case, you can adjust the number of stitches accordingly.

Oops! How Do I Fix That?

Sometimes when a garment is totally finished you will realize that everything is not quite as it should be. The edges may not be even or your foundation chain may be too tight and the garment is pulling at the bottom edge. Here are a few tricks that can fix some common problems.

TOO TIGHT FOUNDATION CHAIN

If you have chained too tightly and the bottom of your garment is pulling, you can, with a little patience, remove the chain and single crochet a new edge. Cut the first stitch, then work your way carefully across the row, taking out one stitch at a time, and working a single crochet in the free loop.

UNEVEN EDGES

As you prepare to sew your garment together, or to pick up stitches on the front edge, you might discover that your edges are so uneven it makes sewing or picking up stitches difficult. You can correct this by working a row of stitches along the edge, using combinations of single crochet, half double crochet and double crochet, filling in uneven spaces as you go.

WEAVING IN THE ENDS

Weaving in all ends can be tedious, but for your project to be properly finished, it should look just as good on the inside as it does on the outside.

Prepare by leaving long tails as you work. Thread the tail on a yarn needle, and weave the tail into stitches on the wrong side of the garment, working in one direction for a few inches. Then, turn and weave in the opposite direction, weaving into nearby stitches to avoid creating too much bulk.

SHOULDERS STRETCHED

Another common problem with crochet garments is that sometimes the shoulders and back neckline stretch out after wearing or are too loose to begin with which causes the sleeve caps to droop. Reinforcing the area with lace seam binding is a quick fix for this problem. Works like a charm!

Blocking

If you feel your garment needs blocking, lay it on a padded surface and pin it into shape according to the pattern schematics adjusted for your body measurements. Spray it with a fine mist from a spray bottle, then cover it with a towel and allow to dry. Sometimes gentle steaming is needed, but remember NEVER to rest the iron on the crocheted fabric. Rather, place a damp cloth over the garment and skim the iron gently over the press cloth, allowing the steam to penetrate through to the crocheted fabric. Allow the garment to dry completely before moving it.

Cathie's Cropped Top

Cathie, a student in one of my workshops, designed this cute top. I was intrigued by her finishing technique as I had never seen anything quite like it before. Cathie graciously agreed to let me include this technique in my book. The top can be worn several ways, and finishing shows two different collar treatments

SKILL LEVEL
EXPERIENCED

Yarn: Lace

Shown: Aunt Lydia's #10 cotton, 100% Mercerized Cotton, 350 yds/320 m, 4 (5, 6) balls #856 Peacock.

Hook: Steel Hook 7 (1.5 mm) or size to obtain gauge

Gauge: 26 sts and 24 rows in patt = 4" (10 cm)

Notions

Yarn needle

Stitch markers

Ten ½" (12 mm) buttons

Sewing needle and matching sewing thread for buttons

Sizes: Small (Medium, Large)

Finished Bust: 36 (39, 43)" (91.5 [99, 109] cm)

Special Stitches

Back to Front single crochet (bf-sc): Insert hook from back to front in next st, yo, draw yarn through st, yo, draw yarn through 2 lps on hook.

Reduced sample of pattern

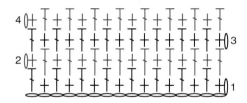

Front

Ch 101 (113, 125) loosely.

Row 1: Sc in 2nd ch from hook (beg ch-2 counts as dc), dc in next ch, *sc in next ch, dc in next ch, rep from * across, turn. (100 [112, 124] sts)

Row 2: Ch 1, sc in first dc, dc in next sc, *sc in next dc, dc in next sc, rep from * across, turn.

Rows 3–6: Rep Row 2.

Row 7 (inc row): Work in patt as established across first 30 (34, 38) sts, 2 sc in next st, sc in next st (mark this st), 2 sc in next st (2 inc made), work in patt across next 34 (38, 42) sts, 2 sc in next st, 1 sc in next st (mark this st), 2 sc in next st (2 inc made), work in patt across last 30 (34, 38) sts. (108 [116, 128] sts)

Rows 8–10: Work even in patt, forming new patt sts over the increased sts, and moving markers up each row.

Row 11 (inc row): Work in patt as established, inc 1 st before and after each marker. (108 [120, 132] sts)

Rows 12–19: [Rep Rows 8–11] twice. (116 [128, 140] sts at end of last row)

Work even in patt until Front measures 7½ (8, 8½)" (19 [20.5, 21.5] cm) from beg.

Shape Armholes

Row 1: Sl st in each of first 11 (12, 13) sts, ch 1, sc2tog over next 2 sts, work in patt as established over next 90 (100, 110) sts, sc2tog over next 2 sts, turn, leaving rem sts unworked. Work even in patt for 1 row. Work in patt as established, dec 1 st at each end of next row, then every 3rd row (7 times), turn. (76 [86, 96] sts)

Work even until armhole measures 4½ (5, 5½)" (11.5 [12.5, 14] cm) from beg.

Right Shoulder

Row 1: Work even in patt across first 12 (13, 14) sts.

Work in patt as established, over these sts only, dec 1 st at neck edge every row (8 times). (4 [5, 6] sts at end of last row) Work even until armhole measures 7½ (8, 8½)" (19 [20.5, 21.5] cm) from beg. Fasten off.

Left Shoulder

Sk center 52 (60, 68) sts, join yarn with sl st in next st, work Left Shoulder same as Right Shoulder, reversing shaping.

Left Back

Note: For the version pictured with only 2 buttons on top, omit buttonholes on Left Back and on Waistband.

Ch 51 (57, 63) loosely.

Work same as Front on 50 (56, 62) sts for 6 rows.

Row 7 (inc row): Work in patt across first 17 sts, 2 sc in next st, sc in next st (mark this st), 2 sc in next st, work in patt across, turn. (52 [58, 64] sts)

Row 8: Work even in patt, forming new patt sts over the increased sts, and moving markers up.

Row 9 (buttonhole row): Work in patt in each of first 3 sts, ch 2, sk next 2 sts, work in patt across, turn.

Row 10: Work in patt across, working 2 sts in ch-2 sp, turn.

Row 11 (inc row): Work in patt as established, inc 1 st before and after marked st, turn. (54 [60, 66] sts)

Move marker up.

Continue working in patt as established, inc 1 st before and after marked st, every 4th row AND AT THE SAME TIME, rep buttonhole row every 8th row until (60 [66, 72] sts) are on work. Then, work even in established patt, still making buttonholes every 8th row until armhole measures 7½ (8, 8½)" (19 [20.5, 21.5] cm) from beg, ending at front edge.

Work in patt across to last 4 (6, 8) sts, turn, leaving rem sts unworked. (56 [60, 64] sts)

Work in patt as established, dec 1 st at armhole end on every other row (15 times), turn. (38 [45, 50] sts) at end of last row

Work even in patt until armhole measures 5½ (6, 6½)" (14 [15, 16.5] cm) from beg.

Left Shoulder

Row 1: Work even in patt across first 12 (13, 14) sts. Work in patt as established, dec 1 st at neck edge every row (8 times) (4 [5, 6] sts at end of last row). Work even until armhole measures 7½ (8, 8½)" (19 [20.5, 21.5] cm) from beg. Fasten off.

Right Back

Work same as Left Back, omit buttonholes. Turn piece over before assembly.

Waistband

Ch 21 loosely.

Row 1: Sc in 2nd ch from hook and in each ch across, turn. (20 sc)

Row 2: Ch 1, bf-sc in each sc across, turn. (20 bf-sc)

Rows 3–4: Rep Rows 1-2.

Row 5 (buttonhole row): Ch 1, sc in each of first 2 sts, ch 2, sk next 2 sts, sc in each of next 9 sts, ch 2, sk next 2 sts, sc in each of last 5 sts, turn.

Row 6: Ch 1, bf-sc sc in each sc across, working 2 sc in each ch-2 space.

Rep Rows 2 and 3 until waistband measures 31 (34, 38)" (79 [86.5, 96.5] cm) from beg, slightly stretched.

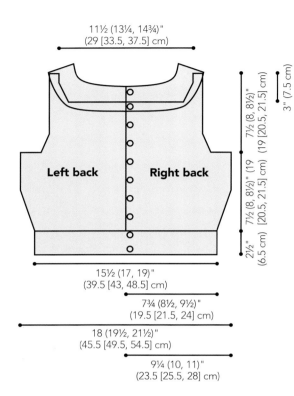

11½ (13¼, 14¾)"
(29 [33.5, 37.5] cm)

Left back   Right back

7½ (8, 8½)"
(19 [20.5, 21.5] cm)

3" (7.5 cm)

7½ (8, 8½)" (19
[20.5, 21.5] cm)

2½"
(6.5 cm)

15½ (17, 19)"
(39.5 [43, 48.5] cm)

7¾ (8½, 9½)"
(19.5 [21.5, 24] cm)

18 (19½, 21½)"
(45.5 [49.5, 54.5] cm)

9¼ (10, 11)"
(23.5 [25.5, 28] cm)

Reduced sample of pattern

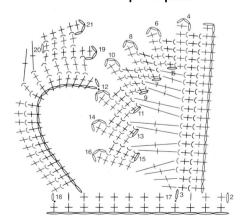

PLAIN COLLAR

Ch 163 (171, 179) loosely.

Row 1: Sc in 2nd ch from hook and in each ch across, turn. (162 [170, 178] sc)

Row 2: Ch 1, bf-sc in each sc across, turn. (162 [170, 178] bf-sc)

Row 3 (inc row): Ch 1, sc in each st across, inc 11 sc evenly space across, turn. (173 [182, 190] sts)

Rows 4–20: Rep Rows 2 and 3 (8 times); then rep Row 2 once, do not turn. Do not fasten off. (261 [270, 278] sts at end of last row)

Button Loops: Working along short end of collar, ch 1, *sk next row, sc in next row-end st*, rep from * to * once, ch 4, rep from * to * 6 times, ch 4, rep from * to * twice. Fasten off.

ARMHOLE TRIM (MAKE 2)

Ch 6 loosely.

Row 1: Sc in 2nd ch from hook and in each ch across, turn. (5 sc)

Row 2: Ch 1, bf-sc in each sc across, turn. (5 bf-sc)

Row 3: Ch 1, sc in each st across, turn. (5 sc)

Rep Rows 2 and 3 until Trim measures 15 (16, 17)" (38 [40.5, 43] cm) from beg. Fasten off.

SCROLL COLLAR

Ch 150 (158, 166) loosely.

Row 1 (WS): Sc in 2nd ch from hook, sc in each ch across row, turn. (149 [157, 165] sc)

Row 2: Ch 1, sc in each of first 2 sc, ch 18, sc in 2nd from hook. Work 19 sc over the ch just made, (20 sc in all), sl st in each of next 2 sc in Row 1, turn.

Row 3: Ch 1, sk next 2 sl sts, working in back loops only, sc in each of next 19 sc, turn, leaving rem sc unworked.

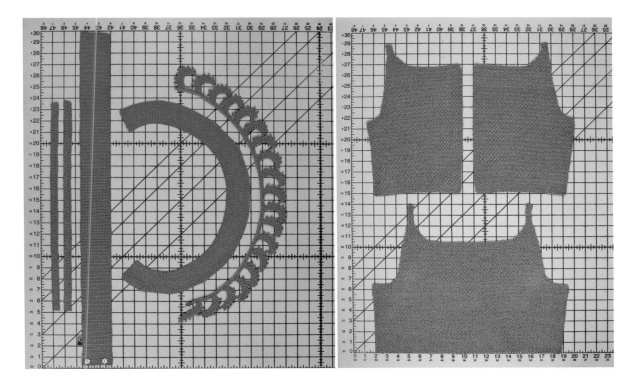

Row 4: Ch 3, sc in 3rd ch from hook (picot made), sc in back loop of each of next 5 sc, turn.

Row 5: Ch 1, sc in back loop of each of next 4 sc, turn, leaving rem sts unworked.

Row 6: Work picot, sc in back loop of each of next 4 sc, sc in back loop of each of next 2 sc, 3 rows below, turn.

Rows 7-16: Rep Rows 5-6 (5 times). At end of Row 16, working in both loops of sts, sc in each of next 2 sc. (7 picots on scroll)

Row 17: Working in both loops of sts, sc in each of next 6 sc on Row 1, ch 17, turn, sl st in 3rd picot from bottom of previous scroll just completed (Row 12), ch 1, turn, work 20 sc over long ch just made, working in both loops of sts, sl st in each of the next 2 sc on Row 1.

Rep Rows 3–17 (16 [17, 18] times); then rep Rows 3–16 once, sc in last sc on Row 1. Fasten off.

FINISHING

Sew shoulder and side seams. Starting and ending at center back edges, sew Waistband evenly across bottom edge of sweater. Without twisting Armhole Trim, sew beg and end of each trim together. Placing seam at underarm, overlapping armhole edge, sew one Armhole Trim around each armhole. Starting and ending at center back edges, overlapping wide edge of Plain Collar or scalloped edge of Scroll Collar ¾" (2 cm) over neck edge of sweater, sew collar to neck edge. With sewing needle and thread, sew buttons to Right Back opposite buttonholes and button loops.

Blocking: Lay garment on a padded surface and sprinkle with water. Pat into shape. Pin out to measurements using rustproof pins. Allow to dry.

SECTION

3

Embellish for Personal Flair

Embellishing a finished garment can mean anything from adding a simple reverse single crochet row to a button band, to adding ruffles and lace trims, to appliquéing some motifs around a neckline and or sleeves. There are some examples of how to do this on the garments shown, but there are many other possibilities. You can also add beads and touches of embroidery for an elegant look. Have fun, experiment, and make every garment special.

Motifs

For a special touch, embellish a sweater with appliquéd motifs. There are several motifs to choose from on the following pages, or you can create your own.

BROAD LEAF

Note: Work leaf on both sides of the foundation chain.

Ch 14.

First half of leaf: 5 tr in 5th ch from hook, 1 tr in each of the next 3 ch, 1 dc in each of the next 2 ch, 1 hdc in each of the next 2 ch, 1 sc in next ch, 1 sl st in last ch, ch 3, sl st in the same ch (point of leaf), do not turn.

Second half of leaf: Working across opposite side of foundation ch, 1 sc in next ch, 1 hdc in each of next 2 ch, 1 dc in each of next 2 ch, 1 tr in each of next 3 ch, 5 tr in last ch, ch 3, Sl st in same ch. Fasten off.

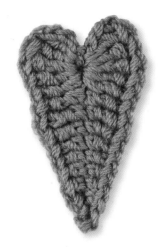
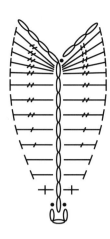

ASTERS

Made with 2 colors: A and B.

Center

Rnd 1 (RS): With A, ch 2, work 8 sc in 2nd ch from hook, join with a sl st in first sc. Fasten off A.

Petals

Rnd 2: With RS facing, join B with a sl st in any sc, [ch 8, sl st] twice in same sc, (sl st [ch 8, sl st] twice) in each sc around, join with sl st in first sc. Fasten off. (16 petals)

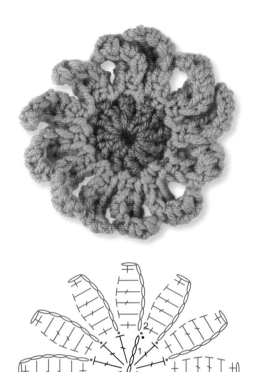

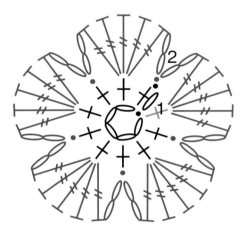

5 PETAL FLOWER

Ch 5, join with a sl st to form a ring.

Rnd 1: Ch 1, 10 sc in ring, join with a sl st to first sc.

Rnd 2: *Ch 2, 5 tr in next sc, ch 2, sl st in next st, rep from * 4 times more. Fasten off.

WILDFLOWER

Made with 2 colors: A and B.

Center

Rnd 1 (RS): With A, ch 1 loosely for center, ch 3 more (counts as dc), work 11 dc in 4th ch from hook, join with a sl st in top of beg ch-4. Fasten off A. (12 dc)

Petals

Rnd 2: With RS facing, join B with a sl st in any dc, *ch 7, sc in 2nd ch from hook, hdc in next ch, dc in each of next 2 ch, hdc in next ch, sc in next ch, sl st in next dc on Center, rep from * around. Fasten off. (12 petals)

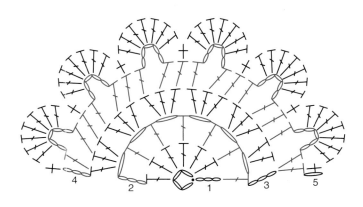

FANCIFUL FAN

The Fanciful Fan can be made in one color, or you may change colors every row.

Note: Though the Fan begins with a ring, all subsequent rows are worked back and forth.

Ch 5, join with a sl st to form a ring.

Row 1: Ch 3 (counts as dc here and throughout), 6 dc in ring, turn. (7 dc)

Row 2: Ch 4 (counts as dc, ch 1), (dc, ch 1) in each of next 5 dc, dc in top of tch, turn. (6 ch-1 sps)

Row 3: Ch 3, 2 dc in first ch-1 sp, 3 dc in each ch-1 sp across, turn. (18 dc)

Row 4: Ch 3, dc in first st, *ch 5, dc in each of next 3 dc; rep from * 4 times, ch 5, sk next dc, 2 dc in top of tch, turn. (6 ch-5 loops)

Row 5: Ch 1, *7 dc in the ch-5 loop, skip next dc, sc in next dc; rep from * 5 times, ending with last sc in top of tch. Fasten off.

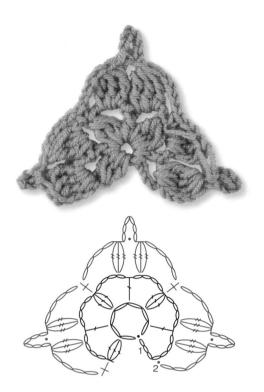

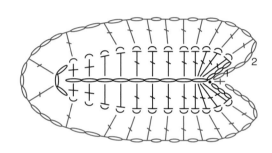

OPEN EDGE LEAF

Note: Work leaf on both sides of the foundation chain.

Ch 12.

Row 1: 4 dc in 4th ch from hook, dc in each of the next 4 ch, hdc in each of the next 2 ch, sc in next ch, (sc, ch 3, sc) in the last ch (point of leaf). Working across opposite side of foundation ch, sc in next ch, hdc in each of next 2 ch, dc in each of the next 4 ch, 5 dc in next ch, ch 3, sl st in the same st as last dc. Do not join to beg of rnd, do not turn, continue around leaf.

Row 2: Ch 5. Working in back loops only, dc in next dc, (ch 1, dc) in each of next 8 sts, ch 2, sk next 2 sts, dc in next st, ch 3, (dc, ch 3, dc) in ch-3 sp at point of leaf. Working on other side of leaf, ch 3, dc in next st, ch 2, sk next 2 sts, dc in next st, (ch 1, dc) in each of next 8 sts, ch 5, sc in base of beg ch-5.

TRIPLE CLUSTER

dc-cluster: *[Yo, insert hook in next st, yo, draw yarn through st, yo, draw yarn through 2 loops on hook] 3 times, yo, draw yarn through 4 loops on hook.*

tr-cluster: **Yo (twice), insert hook in next st, yo, draw yarn through st, [yo, draw through 2 loops on hook] twice; rep from * twice in same st or sp, yo, draw yarn through 4 loops on hook.*

picot: *Ch 6, sl st in 6th ch from hook.*

Ch 6, join with a sl st to form a ring.

Rnd 1 (RS): Ch 7 (counts as dc, ch 4), *dc in ring, ch 4, dc–cluster in ring, ch 4; rep from * once; rep from * to **, once. Fasten off. (3 clusters, 6 ch-4 sps).

Rnd 2: With RS facing, join yarn with a sl st in first ch-4 sp, *ch 4, tr-cluster in ch-4 sp, work picot, tr-cluster in next ch-4 sp, ch 4, sc in next dc-cluster; rep from * twice. Fasten off.

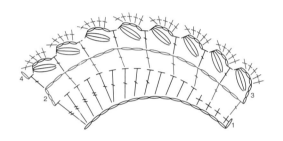
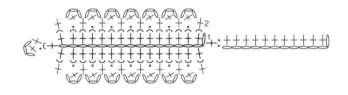

SIDE PUFF LAZY J

Side Puff Stitch (side puff): *Ch 3, [yo and pick up a loop around post of dc just made] 3 times, yo and draw yarn through 6 loops on hook, yo and draw yarn through last 2 loops on hook.*

Ch 16.

Row 1: Sc in 2nd ch from hook, sc in each of the next 3 ch, hdc in each of next 4 ch, dc in each of next 3 ch, 2 dc in next ch, tr in each of the next 2 ch, 2 tr in last ch, turn.

Row 2: Ch 5 (counts as dc, ch 2 here and throughout), sk first 2 sts, dc in next st, [ch 2, sk next 2 sts, dc in next st] 7 times, turn. (8 ch-2 sps)

Row 3: Ch 5, *dc in next dc, work side puff; rep from * 6 times, work side puff, tr in 3rd ch of beg ch-5, turn.

Row 4: Ch 1, 5 sc in each ch-3 sp across, sc in 5th ch of the beg ch-5. Fasten off.

CURLY EDGE LEAF

Picot: *Ch 3, sc in 3rd ch from hook.*

Ch 16.

Row 1: 1 sc in 2nd ch from hook, 1 sc in each of the next 13 ch, 3 sc in the last ch. Working across opposite side of foundation ch, 1 sc in each ch across, 1 sc in tch. Do not join, do not turn.

Row 2: Continue working in a spiral, working in the back loops of sts, *sc in next st, [picot, sl st in next st, sc in next st] 7 times (7 picots)*, [sc in next st, picot, sl st] in next st (point of leaf made). Working on other side of leaf, rep from * to * across, sl st in next st, ch 12 for stem, 1 sc in 2nd chain from hook, 1 sc in each ch across, sl st in next sc at base of leaf. Fasten off.

Edgings

Adding an edging to a garment is a good way to expess your personal style. Edgings can be worked separately and sewn on, or crocheted directly onto the edge to be embellished.

Sew-On Edgings

These edgings are made separately and sewn on. Measure carefully and pin the edging in place before sewing.

NEAPOLITAN LACE

Note: Work from the narrow end.

Ch 5.

Row 1: [3 dc, ch 3, 3 dc] in 5th ch from hook (shell made), turn.

Row 2: Ch 3, shell in next ch-3 sp of previous shell, turn.

Row 3: Rep Row 2.

Row 4: Ch 5, shell in next ch-3 sp of previous shell, turn.

Row 5: Ch 3, shell in next ch-3 sp of previous shell, [ch 2, 1 dc] 6 times in next ch-5 sp, 1 sc in next ch-3 sp, turn.

Row 6: Ch 3, 2 dc in next ch-2 sp, [sl st, ch 3, 2 dc] in each of next 4 ch-2 sps, 1 sc in next ch-2 sp (before shell), ch 3, shell in ch-3 sp of next shell, turn.

Row 7: Rep Row 2.

Rep Rows 4–7 for desired length, ending with Row 6 of pattern. Fasten off.

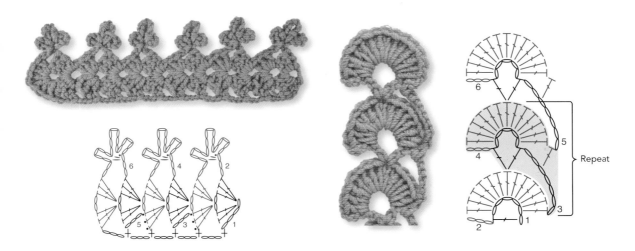

TREFOIL EDGE

Row 1 (WS): Ch 4 (counts as 1 dc, ch 1), [2 dc, ch 2, 3 dc] in 4th ch from hook, turn.

Row 2: Ch 8, sl st in 6th ch from hook, ch 7, sl st in same ch as last sl st, ch 5, sl st in same ch as last sl st (trefoil completed), ch 2, [3 dc, ch 2, 3 dc] in next ch 2 sp, turn.

Row 3: Sl st in each of first 3 dc, ch 3 (counts as a dc), [2 dc, ch 2, 3 dc] in next ch-2 sp, turn.

Rep Rows 2 and 3 until edging is required length, ending with Row 2 of pattern, do not turn.

Edging Row: *Ch 3, 1 sc in top of row-end st, rep from * across, ending with 1 sc in the top of beg ch 4. Fasten off.

SOHO SHELLS

Row 1: Ch 6, dc in 6th chain from hook, turn.

Row 2: Ch 3 (counts as dc here and throughout), 13 dc in ch-5 sp, turn.

Row 3: Ch 7, sk first 6 dc, (dc, ch 5, dc) in next dc, turn.

Row 4: Ch 3, 13 dc in ch-5 sp, dc in next ch-7 loop, turn.

Row 5: Ch 7, sk first 7 dc, (dc, ch 5, dc) in next dc, turn.

Repeat Rows 4 and 5 for desired length of trim, ending with Row 4. Fasten off.

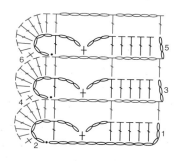

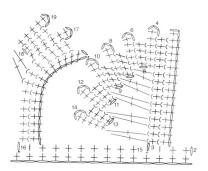

VENETIAN TRIM

Note: Work from the narrow end.

Ch 14.

Row 1: 1 dc in 4th ch from hook, 1 dc in each of the next 4 ch, ch 3, sk next 2 ch, 1 sc in next ch, ch 3, sk next 2 ch, [1 dc, ch 5, 1 sl st] in last ch, turn.

Row 2: [1 sc, 2 hdc, 5 dc] in first ch-5 sp, 1 dc in next dc, ch 5, sk next 2 ch-3 sps, 1 dc in next dc, ch 5, sk next 4 dc, 1 dc in top of tch, turn.

Row 3: Ch 3 (counts as first dc), 4 dc in next ch-5 sp, 1 dc in next dc, ch 3, 1 sc in next ch-5 sp, ch 3, [1 dc, ch 5, 1 Sl st] in next dc, turn.

Rep Rows 2 and 3 for pattern.

IRISH SCROLL

Ch a multiple of 10 plus 3.

Row 1: Sc in 2nd ch from hook, sc in each ch across row, turn.

Row 2: Ch 1, sc in each of first 2 sc, ch 15, sc in 2nd ch from hook. Work 15 sc over the ch just made, (16 sc in all), sl st in each of next 2 sc in Row 1, turn.

Row 3: Ch 1, sk next 2 sl sts, working in back loops only, sc in each of next 15 sc, turn, leaving rem sc unworked.

Row 4: Ch 3, sc in 3rd ch from hook (picot made), sc in back loop of each of next 5 sc, turn.

Row 5: Ch 1, sc in back loop of each of next 4 sc, turn, leaving remaining sts unworked.

Row 6: Work picot, sc in back loop of each of next 4 sc, sc in back loop of each of next 2 sc, 3 rows below, turn.

Rows 7–14: [Rep Rows 5 and 6] 4 times. (6 picots on scroll)

Row 15: Working in both loops of sts, sc in each of next 8 sc on Row 1, ch 15, turn, sl st in 3rd picot from bottom of previous scroll just completed (Row 10), ch 1, turn, work 15 sc over long ch just made, working in both loops of sts, sl st in each of the next 2 sc on Row 1.

Rep Rows 3–15 until 10 sc remain on Row 1; then rep Rows 3–14 once. Fasten off.

Picked Up Edgings

The following edgings can also be crocheted separately and sewn on, if you wish; but because of the way they are constructed, they also work very well when you crochet them directly to the garment. To do this, use the edge row of the garment in place of the foundation chain and begin with Row 1.

SABRINA'S LACE

Dtr2tog: *Yo 3 times, pick up a loop in designated stitch, [yo, draw yarn through 2 loops on hook] 3 times, rep from * once, yo, draw through 3 loops on hook.*

Note: At the end of Row 1, the number of ch-1 spaces must be a multiple of 8 plus 1, in order for the pattern to work out correctly.

Ch a multiple of 16 plus 6.

Row 1: 1 dc in 6th ch from hook, *ch 1, sk next ch, 1 dc in next ch, rep from * across, turn.

Row 2: Ch 3 (counts as first dc now and throughout), [1 dc in next sp, 1 dc in next dc] twice, *ch 5, sk next 2 ch-1 sps, 1 tr in next ch-1 sp, ch 5, sk 2 dc, 1 dc in next dc, [1 dc in next sp, 1 dc in next dc] 3 times (7 dc in group),

rep from * across to within last 2 ch-1 sps, [1 dc in next dc, 1 dc in next ch-1 sp] twice, 1 dc in 3rd ch of tch, turn.

Row 3: Ch 3, sk first dc, 1 dc in each of next 3 dc, *ch 7, 1 sc in next tr, ch 7, sk next dc**, 1 dc in each of next 5 dc, rep from * across, ending last rep at **, 1 dc in each of next 3 dc, 1 dc in top of tch, turn.

Row 4: Ch 3, sk first dc, 1 dc in each of next 2 dc, *ch 7, [1 sc, ch 5, 1 sc] in next sc, ch 7, sk next dc, 1 dc in each of next 3 dc, rep from * across, 1 dc in top of tch, turn.

Row 5: Ch 6 (counts as dc, ch 3), *[dtr2tog, ch 3] 5 times in next ch-5 sp, sk next dc, dc in next dc, ch 3, rep from * across, ending with last 1 dc in top of tch, turn.

Row 6: Sl st in first ch-3 sp, ch 1, 1 sc in same sp, *[ch 5, 1 sc] in each of next 5 sps**, 1 sc in next sp, rep from * across, ending last rep at **, sl st in top of tch. Fasten off.

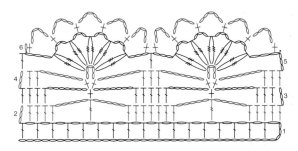

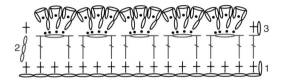

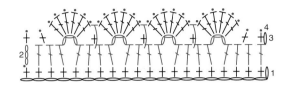

COCK'S COMB

Ch a multiple of 3.

Row 1 (RS): Sc in 2nd ch from hook and in each ch across, turn.

Row 2: Ch 3 (counts as dc), dc in next sc, *ch 1, sk next sc, dc in each of next 2 sc; rep from * across, turn.

Row 3: Ch 1, sc in first dc, *([sl st, ch 4, sl st in 3rd ch from hook for picot] 3 times in same sp, sl st) in next ch-1 sp; rep from * across, sk last dc, sc in top of tch. Fasten off.

BI-COLOR ARCH

Made with 2 colors: A and B.

With A, ch a multiple of 4 plus 1.

Row 1 (RS): With A, sc in 2nd ch from hook, sc in each ch across, turn. Fasten off A.

Row 2: With WS facing, join B with a sl st in first st, ch 3 (counts as dc), sk first sc, dc in each of next 3 sc, *ch 3, dc in each of the next 4 sc; rep from * across, turn.

Row 3: Ch 1, sc in first dc, *sc between 2nd and 3rd dc of 4-dc group**, 6 dc in next ch-3 sp; rep from * across, ending last rep at **, sc in top of tch, do not turn. Fasten off B.

Row 4: With RS facing, join A with a sl st in first st, ch 1, sl st in first sc, *sl st in each of next 6 dc**, working over sc, hdc in sp between 2 dc 2 rows below; rep from * across, ending last rep at **, sl st in each of last 2 sts. Fasten off.

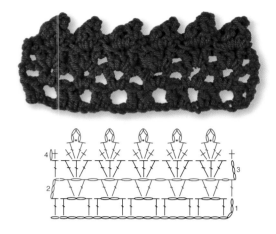

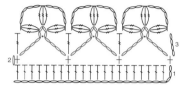

PRINCESS PICOTS

Ch a multiple of 4.

Row 1: 1 dc in 4th ch from hook, *ch 2, sk next 2 ch, 1 dc in each of next 2 ch, rep from * across, turn.

Row 2: Ch 4 (counts as dc, ch 1), *[1 dc, ch 1, 1 dc] in next ch-2 sp (V-st made), ch 1, rep from * across, 1 dc in top of tch, turn.

Row 3: Ch 3 (counts as first dc), *sk next ch-1 sp, 3 dc in ch-1 sp of next V-st, rep from * across, 1 dc in 3rd ch of tch, turn.

Row 4: Ch 1, 1 sc in first dc, *, [1 sc, 1 dc, ch 4, sl st in 4th ch from hook (picot made), 1 dc, 1 sc] in center dc of next 3-dc group, rep from * across, 1 sc in top of tch. Fasten off.

THREE-PETAL SCALLOP

Tr3tog: *Yo twice, pick up a loop in designated stitch [yo, draw through 2 loops on hook] twice, rep from * twice in same stitch, yo, draw through all 4 loops on hook.*

Ch a multiple of 7 plus 3.

Row 1: 1 dc in 4th ch from hook, 1 dc in each ch across row, turn.

Row 2: Ch 1, 1 sc in first dc, *ch 8, sl st in 4th ch from hook (picot made), ch 4, sk next 6 dc, 1 sc in next dc, rep from * across, ending with last sc in top of tch, turn.

Row 3: Ch 4, *[tr3tog, ch 5, tr3tog, ch 5, tr3tog] in next picot, 1 tr in next sc, rep from * across.

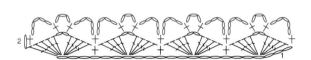

SHELLS AND PICOTS

Ch a multiple of 6 plus 4.

Row 1: Work (4 dc, ch 2, 4 dc) in 4th ch from hook (beg ch 3 counts as dc), *sk next 2 ch, sc in next ch, sk next 2 ch, (4 dc, ch 2, 4 dc) in next ch; rep from * across, ending with 1 more dc in last ch, turn.

Row 2: Ch 1, sc in first dc, *ch 5, (sc, ch 3, sc) in next ch-2 sp, ch 5, sk next 4 dc**, sc in next sc; rep from * across, ending last rep at **, sc in top of tch. Fasten off.

CONTESSA RUFFLE

Note: When picked up along the edges of a garment, this stitch makes a lovely ruffled edge.

Ch a multiple of 3 plus 2.

Row 1: Sc in 2nd ch from hook, sc in next ch, *ch 10, dc in each of the next 3 ch; rep from * across to last 2 ch, ch 10, sc in each of last 2 ch, turn.

Row 2: Ch 3 (counts as dc), dc in next sc, *ch 12, 2 dc in next dc, dc in next dc, 2 dc in next dc; rep from * across to last 2 sts, ch 12, dc in each of last 2 sc. Fasten off.

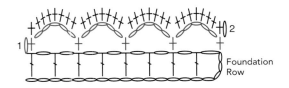

Foundation
Row

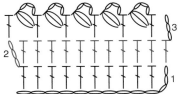

SIMPLE SCALLOP

Ch a multiple of 4.

Foundation Row: 1 dc in 6th ch from hook, *ch 1, sk next ch, 1 dc in next ch, rep from * across, turn.

Row 1: Ch 1, 1 sc in first dc, *ch 5, sk next dc, 1 sc in next dc, rep from * across to within last dc, ch 5, sk next dc, sk next ch, 1 sc in next ch, turn.

Row 2: Ch 1, 1 sc in first sc, 7 sc in each ch-5 loop across, 1 sc in the last sc. Fasten off.

SIDE PUFF SCALLOP

Side Puff Stitch (side puff): *Ch 3, [yo and pick up a loop around post of dc just made] 3 times, yo and draw yarn through 6 loops on hook, yo and draw yarn through last 2 loops on hook.*

Ch a multiple of 2.

Row 1: Dc in 3rd ch from hook, dc in each ch across, turn.

Row 2: Ch 3 (counts as a dc here and throughout), dc in first st, dc in each dc across, working last dc in top of turning ch, turn.

Row 3: Ch 3, dc in next dc, *work side puff, sk next dc, dc in next dc; rep from * across, ending with last dc in top of tch. Fasten off.

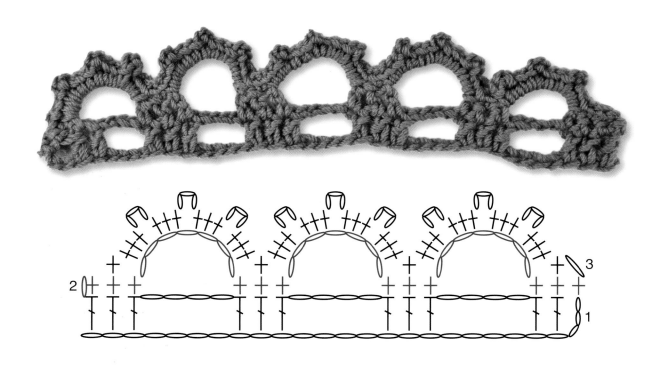

PETITE CROWNS

Ch a multiple of 7 plus 5.

Row 1: Dc in 4th ch from hook, dc in next ch, *ch 4, sk next 4 ch, dc in each of next 3 ch; rep from * across, turn.

Row 2: Ch 1, sc in each of first 3 dc, *ch 7, sk next ch-4 space, sc in each of next 3 dc; rep from * across, ending with last sc in top of tch, turn.

Row 3: Ch 1, sk first sc, sc in next sc, ([3 sc, ch 3] 3 times, 3 sc) in next ch-7 loop, sk next sc, sc in next sc; rep from * across. Fasten off.

BI-COLOR CABLE

Worked with 2 colors: A and B.

Note: Can be worked on an edge of sc, dc or tr.

Row 1 (RS): With A, ch 1, sc in each of first 2 sts, *ch 3, sk next 2 sts, sc in next st, rep from * across to last st, sc in last st, do not turn. Fasten off.

Row 2: With RS facing, join B with sl st in first sc of Row 1, ch 1, sc in first st, *ch 3, remove loop from hook, insert hook from front to back in ch-3 sp of previous row, pick up dropped loop and draw through the ch-3 sp; rep from * across to last ch-3 sp, ch 3, sk next st, sc in last st. Fasten off.

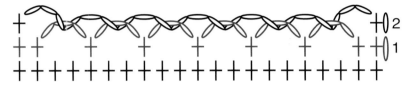

RUFFLE EDGE

When last row of piece to be embellished is completed, ch 3 turn, 1 sc in first st, * ch 3, 1 sc in next st. Repeat from * along entire edge to be embellished.

Pockets

Add pockets to any of the sweaters, following these instructions. Both styles are fairly inconspicuous, but they may add visual weight to the lower third of the sweater, which can be beneficial for an inverted triangle body type.

Patch pocket

Patch Pocket

Most crocheted garments use patch pockets because it is very easy to make a square of the required size, in any pattern that you happen to be using. Just pin the pocket in place and sew it to the outside of the front.

Set-in Pockets

The set-in pocket is worked a little differently. Make your pocket lining first, and set it aside. Begin the front of your garment and work up to the level of the pocket opening, ending with a wrong-side row. Then insert the pocket as follows:

1 Pin the lining to the back of the work at the pocket location, with the upper edge even with the top of the work.

2 Work across the front to the edge of the pocket lining. Then work across the upper edge of the lining, thus joining the lining to the front piece.

3 Skip the same number of stitches on the front as are on the pocket lining, then work the remaining front stitches.

4 Work the remaining rows of the front, following the garment pattern.

5 Sew the pocket lining to the back of the garment piece so the stitches are invisible from the front.

Set-in pocket front

Set-in pocket back

Set-in pocket opened

Buttonholes

In crocheted garments, buttonholes can be vertical or horizontal, but they always lie parallel to the rows. Horizontal buttonholes are worked into the body of the front; vertical buttonholes are crocheted into button bands. To add buttonholes to a garment that doesn't have them included in the instructions, be sure you also adjust the width of the fronts to allow for the overlap. Mark the location of each buttonhole. Then, when you come to a mark, on the first row, make a chain of a few stitches (depending on the size of the button), skip over the same number of stitches and continue. Then on the return row, stitch into the chains at each buttonhole.

Vertical Buttonholes

Horizontal Buttonholes

Covered Buttons

Crocheted button covers are the ideal solution when you can't find the perfect buttons for your cardigan. Made with the same yarn as the sweater, they are always guaranteed to match! Or crochet them from a matching or coordinating color yarn in a lighter weight for a finer appearance. Use plain shank buttons as the base, and, for best results, crochet the covers using a hook size slightly smaller than the hook recommended for the yarn weight. The stitches will be denser for better coverage.

Here's how:

Foundation: Ch 4, sl st to first ch to form ring.

Rnd 1 (RS): Ch 1, work 8 sc in ring, sl st to first st to join. Do not turn.

Rnd 2: Ch 1, 2 sc in each st around. (16 sc)

If the cover is not about the same diameter as the button, work another rnd, increasing every other st.

Last rnd: Ch 1, 1 sc in each st around. Fasten off, leaving a 12" (30.5 cm) tail of yarn for sewing. Thread tail onto yarn needle. Place button inside "cup" of button cover and, using yarn needle, catch outside loops of last row, and draw up tightly to enclose button inside cover and knot. Use remaining yarn to sew button in place.

Button Collar

Add a little frill to your cardigan with ruffled button collars. Use the same yarn and hook as for your project.

Foundation: Ch 10, join with a sl st to form a ring.

Rnd 1: Ch 1, 12 sc in center of ring, join with a sl st to beg ch 1.

Rnd 2: Working from the back loop only, 1 sc in first sc, [ch 3, 1 sc next sc] 11 times, ch 3, join with a sl st to beg sc, fasten off. (12 ch-3 loops)

Zipper Closure

Your pattern may call for buttons but you prefer a zipper closure. Omit the instructions for crocheting overlapping button bands, and instead make two fronts with edges that meet. If you prefer, add an edging, such as reverse single crochet.

When you insert a zipper into a garment seam, you want the garment edges to close over the zipper teeth, but still allow the zipper to operate freely. Follow these steps for properly inserting a zipper:

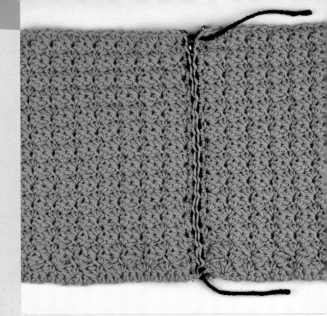

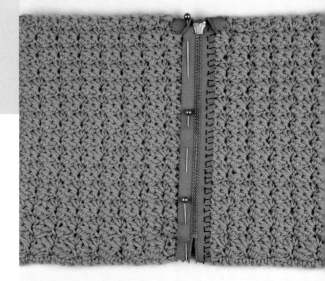

1. Baste the garment edges together with a contrasting thread, using the weave seam method (opposite).

2. Center the zipper face down over the seam on the wrong side of the garment. Pin the zipper in place along both sides of the teeth.

3. Using matching thread, hand stitch the zipper to the garment using a running stitch down the center of each side, and then whipstitch the edges. By catching only the inner layer of the crocheted fabric, the zipper insertion will be nearly invisible from the right side. Turn back the tape ends at the top of the zipper and stitch them in place.

4. Remove the basting stitches from the right side.

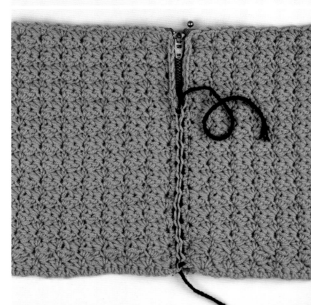

Shoulder Pads

Sometimes use of a small shoulder pad can help balance narrow shoulders and wider hips. Here's how to make shoulder pads:

1 Crochet a small square, using the same yarn as your garment, even the same stitch, if you prefer.

2 Fold the square diagonally forming a triangle. Stitch the edges together.

3 Center the pad over the shoulder seam with the long edge along the sleeve seam and the square corner pointing toward the neckline. Tack it in place along the shoulder seam.

Our Models

Nicole Valencia

Brittany DeLaBarrera

Jeanne Hudson

Sharon Hubert Valencia

Abbreviations

Here is the list of standard abbreviations used for crochet.

approx	approximately		oz	ounce(s)
beg	begin/beginning		p	picot
bet	between		patt	pattern
BL	back loop(s)		pc	popcorn
bo	bobble		pm	place marker
BP	back post		prev	previous
BPdc	back post double crochet		rem	remain/remaining
BPsc	back post single crochet		rep	repeat(s)
CC	contrasting color		rev	sc reverse single crochet
ch	chain		rnd(s)	round(s)
ch-	refers to chain or space previously made, e.g., ch-1 space		RS	right side(s)
ch lp	chain loop		sc	single crochet
ch-sp	chain space		sc2tog	single crochet 2 stitches together
CL	cluster(s)		sk	skip
cm	centimeter(s)		sl st	slip stitch
cont	continue		sp(s)	space(s)
dc	double crochet		st(s)	stitch(es)
dc2tog	double crochet 2 stitches together		tbl	through back loop(s)
dec	decrease/decreases/decreasing		tch	turning chain
dtr	double treble or triple		tfl	through front loop(s)
FL	front loop(s)		tog	together
foll	follow/follows/following		tr	treble or triple crochet
FP	front post		trtr	triple treble crochet
FPdc	front post double crochet		tr2tog	treble or triple crochet 2 stitches together
FPsc	front post single crochet		WS	wrong side(s)
g	gram(s)		yd	yard(s)
hdc	half double crochet		yo	yarn over
inc	increase/increases/increasing		[ ]	Work instructions within brackets as many times as directed
lp(s)	loop(s)		( )	Work instructions within parentheses as many times as directed
Lsc	long single crochet		*	Repeat instructions following the single asterisk as directed
m	meter(s)			
MC	main color		* *	Repeat instructions between asterisks as many times as directed or repeat from a given set of instructions
mm	millimeter(s)			

Stitch Symbols

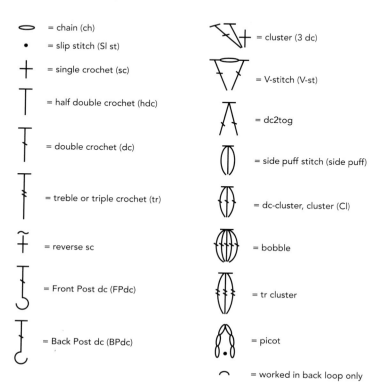

⬯	= chain (ch)
•	= slip stitch (Sl st)
✝	= single crochet (sc)
⊤	= half double crochet (hdc)
⊤	= double crochet (dc)
	= treble or triple crochet (tr)
	= reverse sc
	= Front Post dc (FPdc)
	= Back Post dc (BPdc)

	= cluster (3 dc)
	= V-stitch (V-st)
	= dc2tog
	= side puff stitch (side puff)
	= dc-cluster, cluster (Cl)
	= bobble
	= tr cluster
	= picot
⌒	= worked in back loop only

Term Conversions

Crochet techniques are the same universally, and everyone uses the same terms. However, US patterns and UK patterns are different because the terms denote different stitches. Here is a conversion chart to explain the differences.

US	UK
single crochet (sc)	double crochet (dc)
half double crochet (hdc)	half treble crochet (htr)
double crochet (dc)	treble (tr)
treble or triple crochet (tr)	double treble (dtr)

ADJUST TO FIT • EMBELLISH TO TASTE

Customize
YOUR CROCHET

Margaret Hubert

Creative Publishing
international

Dedication

To my wonderful family.

Acknowledgments

Thanks to **Cathie Nolan** for allowing me to use her original design and **Red Heart Yarns** who provided the yarn for Cathie's Cropped Top.

I also would like to thank **Paula Alexander, Jeannine Buehler, Theresa DeLaBarrera,** and **Nancy Smith,** who helped crochet all the beautiful garments.

Thanks to **Sharon Hubert Valencia,** my daughter; **Nicole Valencia,** my granddaughter; **Brittany DeLaBarrera,** and **Jeanne Hudson** for modeling.

Last, but certainly not least, a very big thank you to my wonderful editor, **Linda Neubauer.** With every new book we work on together, Linda manages, with much patience, to teach me some new bit of technology to help me work more efficiently.

It takes a lot of people to put a book together, from the making of all the garment sections, the photography, and the editing to the yarn companies who so generously donated their yarn and all the behind the scenes staff.

I owe special thanks to:

Lion Brand Yarn Company, who provided all the yarn for 16 garments in the book.

Chris Hubert, my son, who did all the photography, working with me every week for months.

Karen Manthey for her extraordinary diagrams and tech editing.

Singer Sewing Company, who provided their wonderful adjustable dress form, an invaluable tool when making garments.

Guardian Custom Products for providing their E-Z Blocking Board, on which all the garment pieces are shown. Every crocheter should own one of these.